NEW YORK REVIEW BOO

POETS

MELISSA MONROE t
Research in New York. H(
Language, was published in 199,, and the
verse, *On Trepanation and Human Nature: Perspectives from
Paul Broca to the Present*, was published in 2014.

Melissa Monroe

Medusa Beach

and Other Poems

NYRB/POETS

nyrb　NEW YORK REVIEW BOOKS　*New York*

THIS IS A NEW YORK REVIEW BOOK
PUBLISHED BY THE NEW YORK REVIEW OF BOOKS
435 Hudson Street, New York, NY 10014
www.nyrb.com

Library of Congress Cataloging-in-Publication Data
Names: Monroe, Melissa, author.
Title: Medusa Beach : and other poems / Melissa Monroe.
Description: New York City : New York Review Books, 2020. | Series: New
  York Review Books poets
Identifiers: LCCN 2019058443 (print) | LCCN 2019058444 (ebook) | ISBN
  9781681374581 (paperback) | ISBN 9781681374598 (ebook)
Subjects: LCGFT: Poetry.
Classification: LCC PS3563.O5293 M43 2020 (print) | LCC PS3563.O5293
  (ebook) | DDC 811/.54—dc23
LC record available at https://lccn.loc.gov/2019058443
LC ebook record available at https://lccn.loc.gov/2019058444

ISBN 978-1-68137-458-1
Available as an electronic book; ISBN 978-1-68137-459-8

Cover and book design by Emily Singer

Printed in the United States of America on acid-free paper.
10 9 8 7 6 5 4 3 2 1

Contents

Contingent

On the one hand, one hand
creeping through leaf mold,
ticking off the dead
ends of low bushes
a twig at a time.

It investigates
under spongy
logs, fingering
the fine, hairy moss,
the slimy backs

of red-and-black
salamanders,
tightly rolled
pillbugs, dry seeds,
molted feathers. What it needs

seems to be gone, and what's left
shatters at a touch.
The hand cannot afford
to linger. Too much
to cover. Too late.

Its muscles are sore.
The space under its nails
is clogged with grit
so it no longer feels
as clearly as before.

Not here. Not here.
It overturns
the colored leaves brusquely,
scattering dust.
Puddles are starting to freeze,

and soon the ground will be
impenetrable.
It digs in while it can,
closing around cold clay,
up to its knuckles, but just

scratching the surface.
Disturbed debris
settles down over it.
Now it will curl up tight
into a fist, and wait.

On the other, the other
has taken to the air.
The fingers wiggle
ambiguously.
Daylight flows

between each pair.
It helps itself
to whatever wanders
into its pink, almost
translucent web, although

it no longer knows
what it came here after:
maybe a free ride,
maybe rumors of gold—
unsubstantiated.

The hand is never quite
able to grasp what's right
at its fingertips.
It tries to palm a bit
of wind, but the wind slips

effortlessly away.
Matter is no better.
Motes blow past
by the billions, too fast
to follow. Besides,

the hand is trying to hold
out for something more
resistant, unresolved,
something that isn't there,
but might be, so

it fondles each gust
of blue and white
briefly and
releases it for
another. Unless

an unusually
aggressive breeze
carries it off,
it could easily
hover here forever.

Planetogenesis, Chapter 1
SEVEN EARLY EONS IN A SELF-CREATION MYTH

1. THE IMAGINARY PLANET'S FIRST MORNING

The imaginary planet woke up   early, excited. It could be
whatever it wanted—no limits!   All those other old
planets would see!   It looked out the window.
Still dark. But did it   even need a sun?
That prescriptive, patriarchal,   heliocentric thing
had already been done.... It dozed again.

                                        Its own
system, yes.   Self-illuminated, with nobody else's
gravity dragging it around.   Its own galaxy, or—why not?—
its own whole universe,   where *it* would make the rules:
as many dimensions   as it felt like; it could bend
back over on itself   to do tricks with time, or expand
forever. But for now

                        it was content in the bed.
Everything was so pleasantly   undifferentiated,
empty but full   of infinite potential.
The seeds of all its plans   were still intact,
gathering strength to germinate and break   out of their shells.
Its incipient body lolled   lazily, waiting to be told
what shape to take.

                        So just a little longer, please,
under the warm invisible covers—   just a few
more eons of anticipation.   Soon enough, it knew,
all the alternatives but one   would evaporate.
The alarm would ring.   Or it would be jolted awake
by the crashes and whistles   of the garbage men
working their way   from building to building.

2. THE IMAGINARY PLANET ACQUIRES THE BASICS

In Earth Science class   the imaginary planet
learned about the elements;   its future would depend
largely on how much of which   went into it.
At any given temperature and pressure   should it be mostly
solid, liquid, or gas?   How much metal? How conductive,
how reactive, how stable?

                        The real planets spent recess
chasing each other around the playground.   Idiots.
But they didn't have a choice   about what they were made of:
boring ordinary elements with low   atomic numbers, so
what could you expect?   It sat alone,
studying the patterns in the periodic table,   trying to decide
on its own composition:

                        well-balanced, nothing flashy
(no extravagant lodes of gold),   but distinctive—not just
the standard setup: core, mantles, crust.   Maybe it could skip
the solid phase completely, and flow   all over itself in unstoppable
waves. Or maybe   it would have lots of pockets, like a cheese,
and fill them   with titanium, xenon, krypton,
and other secret weapons.

                      Super-density
would be useful. It could see itself   with an excited neon surface
glowing like a tangerine,   and underneath, as-yet-untapped, prodigious,
plutonic energies. . . .   What if one day
a big, greedy hand   went on the rampage through the galaxies,
plucking all the puny, terrified   planets out of their orbits?
Yes!

        Here it comes, ripping through the atmosphere,
reaching eagerly for   what looks like a delicious prize!
Little does it know   that the imaginary planet's mass is vast
and its heat the heat   of a million million suns.
The fingers close, then—   spring open, writhing in pain!

The evil hand flees,   and all the planets, free again,
bounce around the firmament,   cheering their hero.

3. THE IMAGINARY PLANET WORKS ON ITS FORM

The imaginary planet   was trying its best
to be different   from the real ones, but the project
was harder than it had expected.   It designed a new kind
of smooth, looping hill   but the prototypes looked
inescapably like   soft-serve ice-cream cones.
That wasn't what it had in mind.

                                        Shelve the hills for now.
How would it handle water?   No oceans. Everyone had oceans,
and even Mars   probably had rivers.
What about a sort of lake   but not sunken, *above*
ground level, and instead of   liquid, vapor?
Better! It was beautiful!   It was diaphanous, ethereal. . . . It—
Shit. It was just a cloud.

                              Maybe water itself
was a hopeless cliché.   Should it go for a minimalist,
perfectly uniform,   reflective surface?
Too slick, too obvious.   It would start with something small
and work up from there.   What were the essential
properties of trees?   If it could eliminate these,
it would be original. But wait.

                              It remembered the lake.
All right, it would eliminate *some*   and change the others
just enough   to create something still identifiable,
yet all its own.   It drafted a terrific tree—
no trunk, no branches,   just one titanic leaf, tethered
to the ground by a long, long silky-strong   spider's-web stem.
Not a kite. Not at all—

complex, alive, fully equipped
to photosynthesize. The planet dashed off   a dozen, in all colors,
and basked proudly in their shade.   But then the first one drooped,
and the second, and—   It cursed itself. Of course!
How could it have a forest   without earth, water, or air?
It ripped down all the shimmering leaves before   any more could
     wither
and went back to kneading its lump   of ugly gray clay.

4. THE IMAGINARY PLANET CONSIDERS ITS OPTIONS

Everybody always asked the imaginary planet   why
it insisted on being imaginary.   Its standard reply—
that that was just the way it was—   was brushed aside.
Some thought it simply   needed encouragement.
Others called it perverse.   Several had the nerve
to suggest a therapist.
                              They never seemed to tire
of enumerating the advantages   of being real:
official recognition   in all the textbooks;
eligibility   for federal funding if you proved to be
a suitable candidate   for exploration; maybe even
a spot on educational TV.   The imaginary planet withdrew
to deep space, and brooded.
                              Everywhere it looked,
real matter was churning itself   into a frenzy.
Hot new stars   condensed, expanded, and burned down to dwarfs.
Countless solar systems   were writhing in the spiral tentacles
of powerful galaxies,   which were gobbled up in turn
by superclusters.   Was the imaginary planet missing out
on all the excitement?
                              The real planets rushed around earnestly,

caught up in their tedious orbits.   A's eclipsing B!
C and D are in conjunction.   Poor E! Its ozone layer
has started thinning badly.   Did you hear that F
finally got that fifth moon certified?   Big goddamn deal.
It could see the appeal of fame,   but being observed
forced you to take positions

                                        you might regret.
It wasn't prepared to commit   to any particular form,
or pledge allegiance   to some pompous gas ball
that called itself a sun.   It didn't want swarms
of roach-like robots   poking their probes
into its crust, or astronauts in silly suits   galumphing across it,
brandishing flags. Besides,

                              every cosmic documentary
seemed to end the same: entropy.
No. It would keep its options open.   It smoothed
its imaginary surface free   of imaginary bootprints,
restored its unspecified perfection,   and spun
along the oscillating   edge of a fresh
possible universe, in frictionless   perpetual motion.

5. THE IMAGINARY PLANET STARTS ITS MENAGERIE

The imaginary planet   wanted lots of pets—
the most, the best, the biggest.   Since it wasn't real,
it wouldn't have to mess   with sticky strings
of nucleotides,   or wait and wait
for desirable traits   to evolve, but it took pride
in its mastery of classical technique.

                                        It could produce
fish every bit as fishy   as traditional fish.
Ornithologists   would be wowed by its complete
collection of finches, each with a distinctive   specialized beak.

14

Its rabbits and chickens and sheep   would win blue ribbons
at the county fair.   And once it had paid its dues,
it would really cut loose,

                          with fauns and griffins,
psammeads and snarks,   and even more marvelous creatures,
never dreamed of before.   For practice, it whipped up a batch
of protoprotozoa and watched them   tentatively extending
pseudopodia to slide   around their petri dish.
Sometimes one would pause   then pull itself in opposite
directions and split.

                    Now it was two.
The planet was pleased   but bored. A colony of single cells
was of limited interest.   It made a warm, comfortable nest
with pillows and towels and bowls,   and spent all night creating
its first masterpiece: a big, beautiful beast
with shaggy fur to cuddle up against,   golden eyes that would stare
reverently at its master,

                          and a wide toothy mouth
that would be grateful to be fed.   The beast gulped down
its dinner in three bites,   peed on everything in sight,
and eviscerated its bed.   It was adorable,
but it seemed unaware   of the planet. It trotted about,
sniffing the air   for pheromonal traces
of another beast, then dug a hole

                              and went to sleep. At least
the little plate of culture   was always ambitiously
multiplying. Maybe in time   it would develop into
something smart enough to wonder who   supplied the medium.
Again and again the tiny nuclei   subdivided, without apparent
ardor or regret,   and the new cells crept
away from their former selves   on their false feet.

6. THE IMAGINARY PLANET'S MIDNIGHT MEDITATIONS

Sometimes stupid ontological   questions kept
the imaginary planet   awake in the middle of the night.
Was the sky in which it floated   imaginary too?
If a real meteor   collides with an imaginary planet, does it
make a sound?   Or does it sail right through,
totally unperturbed?

                        The planet felt more substantial
than that vague, gray soup   beyond its window, bigger and brighter
than the barley stars   or the almost translucent
onion-slice moon. Maybe a snack   would help it relax.
But even the refrigerator   reminded it of how it used to peek
into the crack   of the closing door to see if the light stayed on
when no one was watching.

                        But *it* was watching, so that
didn't prove a thing.   And then it discovered the button,
and all the mystery was gone.   Still—the locked black box,
the chocolate-covered Easter egg,   the geode that you had to smash
to discover the crystal teeth   that had been forming there
all along, like a teratoma. . . .   It liked the idea.
While all the "real"

                    planets (what made them so sure?)
flounced around in their fancy rings,   their oxygen-rich atmospheres,
their myriad life-forms,   the imaginary planet, disguised
in a dingy, inorganic crust,   would be cultivating pearls the size
of baby moons in molten opal lagoons,   and forests of überorchids
whose nectar fed flocks   of tiny dinosaurs
with butterfly wings

                  deep in its secret core.
But was imagining   itself enough? (It tossed, threw off a blanket.)
It had to admit   it still was hoping for
empirical confirmation: Amazing discovery!
Imaginary planet's existence verified!   Unparalleled treasures

anticipated; Nobel Prize   certain, say experts.
At first it would resist

                                   the diamond drill bits and the dynamite,
savoring the corroborative pain,   postponing the moment
when an eternity of pressure   would be released,
and all its unseen   insides would explode outward in
glorious smithereens!   A chorus line of actual angels
would dance an irrefutable   cancan on the head of an
imaginary pin: A-one and a-two, three, four.... The planet slept.

7. THE IMAGINARY PLANET'S LAST RESORT

It occurred to the imaginary planet   that what it needed
might be a human mind   to imagine it.
But how to find one?   Should it place an ad
in *The Village Voice*   or on the Internet?
It studied the listings   and spent many hours
composing an appropriate profile:

                                   "World of Your Own!
Planet, S, attributes   negotiable, seeks
M or F for serious,   nurturing, nontraditional relationship.
Marital status/age/race/weight   unimportant.
No intelligent designers.   Interest in alternate
universes a plus.   I'll be whatever you can dream—
let's collaborate!"

                         The next morning,
its mailbox was full   but the responses
were a big disappointment.   Of course it had known
it would attract some wackos,   but so many?
Most made lewd jokes   about "a Big Bang."
Some included equations   the planet couldn't interpret.
Several long, rambling, nearly illiterate texts

                                   proposed to enlist

the planet in   "the performative transgression
of hegemonic linear discourse."   This sounded dangerous.
The actual suggestions   for physical or cosmological
innovations were all depressingly   old hat or impractical:
seven spheres, dark matter,   Ecotopia, Planet of the Apes.
Delete. Delete. Delete. Delete.
                                   One small, poorly scanned
photo of a brain slice   caught the planet's eye.
All the message said was: "Like what you see?
There's more where this came from."   The planet was not at all certain
that the brain   had really grasped the situation,
but something about those   drab, malleable lobes
seemed sympathetic. It took a deep breath   and clicked Reply.

Bundling—Its Origin, Progress, and Decline in America

(based on the 1871 study by Henry Reed Stiles)

Bundling, defined
in Grose's *Dictionary of the Vulgar Tongue*
as "a man and woman lying
on the same bed with their clothes on," is, despite
persistent sophistic assertions, demonstrably

unconnected with
the infamous *namzat bezé*
of the Afghan, and the "bundling bag," said to encase
each lover like a sausage skin, tied tight
at the chin, is a myth.

No centerboard or post
bisected their berth. Legitimate
historians have paid but little heed
to the japes of the pharisees
who would ascribe

to bundling "the unparalleled increase
in the Yanokie or Yankee tribe."
However, these and kindred misconceptions
abound, and the hour is overdue
to ventilate

the subject, that the breath
of truth dispel
the foul opprobrium which yet today
blackens the fair fame
of the Wooden Nutmeg State. We can trace

this bygone use, under the name
of "kweesting" (thought allied
to "questing" and "quizzing"), in and out
of the bights and armlets and bays
of the Zuider Zee,

where spooning prospective
spouses under down
quilts or ruder covers may or may
not have respected
proprieties, across

various waters, highland heaths,
and into the bituminous recesses
of Cambrian rills.
Everywhere, indeed,
where winter nights and paths

between villages are long, and hearths grow cold,
and prudence and need
militate against the unpardonable
extravagance of heaping after dark
more fuel on the coals,

and canny country folk
subscribe to the ancient adage about buying
pigs in pokes, maids and their sparks
took themselves in openness into
an inner chamber, divested

halfway, by candle flame,
and there perpetuated
wittingly or no, under the counterpane,
a custom reliably dated
to the age of lords and thanes.

Troubadours tell
of how the feudatories sent their sons
to castles where reproachless demoiselles
(as in "Blonde at Oxford") put off
their outer weeds,

pulled curtains that smelled
of dust and tallow,
and welcomed their footsore swains
on beds of pressed
rush or fern. And should we delve

deeplier still
into antiquity, to reach the days when first
the conquering tramp
of legions of sandals
resounded among the aboriginal Angles,

Caesar, censorious,
retails for our derision how the crude, near-brute
natives of Thule
tarried together on the common straw
in their rank hovels,

with nary a blush, "polyandrous
polygamists," amidst
the audible respirations of their kine and swine.
Strabo and Xiphilin likewise
recoiled, but it behooves

the scrupulous modern student to refrain
from remonstrance. In our haste
to vindicate (so we would have it) the spotless
character of our race,
we should not reprove

the innocent Savages of this land, whose chaste
assignations to a strange degree
resembled our olden ways.
Neither should the New
Netherlander set himself above

his country cousins to the north, and blame
the "sturdy barbarians" of Hartford for
their rustic custom. Follow
the cunning Knickerbocker back, and see
the deliberate crack

at the windowsill
wide enough for a hand to slide
under the sash and push. Inside,
his granddame waits
for the clop of mynheer's boots, the brief

scuffle of cloth on brick; a cloaked shape
rises in the casement, fills it. Here the eye
of history circumspectly
winks. What blandishments
were thereupon exchanged

we may readily surmise,
for, though priests and principalities and kings
come and go, dallying
over the centuries well-nigh certainly
remains much the same.

And whether more bastards be
catched in this wise
than any other is perhaps a question
we cannot decide
and thus should not pursue,

nor lend undue
credence to the treatises of travelers unschooled
in local tongues, prepossessed, narrow-souled
and thus but ill
fit to pass sentence. Witless misconstruals

and badinage aside,
the fact that this practice, born of thermal
convenience and love, survived
countless ages almost
without remark

would argue in itself
that the greater part of bundlers better held
the genial current of their souls in check
than do our silk-beribboned
nymphs and their duded

Strephons. The Reverends
Eels and Barnaby, who much inveighed
against the "natural consequences" of their flocks'
nocturnal interviews,
would have been well advised

to turn their attentions to the parlors of the town,
where even as they preached,
milady was beginning to eschew
the elbow chair, and receive her blades
in finery less

restrictive than a village lassie's modest
nightslip, sprawled
voluptuously on a supple
upholstered divan. Researches indicate
that in those "civilized"

precincts where the sofa has been introduced,
rendering courtship more
palatable and Turkish, virtue
relaxes her beneficent embrace, and the rate
of bastardy soars.

And all the animadversions
of the bluenoses and blackcoats, the hue
and cry from the pulpit
notwithstanding, untold
generations continued to "go under

kiver" together, with minimal
appearance of issue. Who dare to call
the maids of old Connecticote depraved
above others of their sex
themselves should shed

the tattered veil
of willful ignorance and contemplate the late
corruption of our commonweal: loose camp
manners and rakish tastes
imported from the Canadian campaigns.

Let them read
the illustrated papers, whose foul sheets unleashed
an undammable tide
of wantonness across our heretofore
continent land.

Here our daughters learned
worldly desires: disdain
for the spindle and needle, lust
for perpetually changing, boughten-made
accouterment. Here the popular muse

incited them to ridicule
their forebears' homespun
wooing, and smothered the outworn observance with scorn
precipitously, and, apparently,
for good and all.

For it was not the thundered
anathemas of the Divines
that finally ended
the trysts. By every evidence, the long
habit of bundling was broken by a song.

An almanac, at the time
widely circulated all about the East, but lost
since then, and now
known only in an incomplete and likely
corrupted broadside version, found

wrapped around a fish slice in a Haddam
attic, attacked
"this vile practice" in rhymes
so facetious and keen
they soon were taken up in every lane.

Letters of the day relate
scenes of mighty raillery—young pairs accused,
upbraided, and shamed
so stingingly, "the slut and clown,"
however pure in fact,

were driven to abstain
thereafter from their newly reprehended
endearments, and bundling became
with each season increasingly
a byword, until

even in the upland dells,
homely wenches turned their backs
on the old-fangled fashions, tricked themselves
out in artless imitation
of city jades, disported on slick

couches of horsehair and brocade,
and presently were sooner seen dead
than bundling. Scarce
a century later, the venerable use
has fallen entirely away,

and we who weigh
contesting testimonies, essaying to winnow
the wholesome truth
from titillating fabrications,
and stoutly defend

our unimpeachable
heritage from knaves and fools, must redouble
our struggle; our foes
are legion, and the conclusion
far from foregone.

The common mind grows
coarser year by year, ever eagerer
to infer the worst.
Moreover, imperceptibly but steadily, our sure
apprehension of the past decays,

and what we know today
perforce relies
on scattered, discrepant allusions, gleaned
from accounts mostly partial
in design, embellished, or based

on misconstructions, and thus of questionable
worth, whence, unless
some blessed twist
of fate restore it to its former favor,
we reluctantly predict

that bundling, save
among the fusty scholiasts whose business
is what once was,
may further fade, surrendering its pure
essence to incorrigible or

innocent error,
darkening in distant retrospect, progressively obscured
by fancy's dirt,
and at length altogether
effaced, lost to the shadowy realm of fable.

Night Patrol

(suggested by Psychology for the Fighting Man—Prepared for the Fighting Man Himself By a Committee of the NATIONAL RESEARCH COUNCIL with the Collaboration of SCIENCE SERVICE as a Contribution to the War Effort, *Washington, A Fighting Forces–Penguin Special, 1943)*

I thought I was well prepared.
I had sat for an hour
in a closet with red
goggles until I could almost read
the labels in the coats.

I had cut the buttons
off my black velvet suit
and peeled the tips from the laces
of my navy blue suede shoes,
so I wasn't afraid

of reflections. My face
was kohled over and I could hide
my teeth behind my lips.
Only the wet whites
of my eyes would give me away.

Gloves, instruments, gun.
I waited inside
until the moon was gone,
then raised the latch without the least
click. Was it clear? No.

The sky was low
and thickly padded.
There was nothing I could do
about the occasional sharp, accurate
star that made it through.

All these gray shapes
belonged to me: my trees,
my trenches, my sandbags, my apparently
empty fields.
I knew my way around

the mines. The captured ground
resisted my feet
softly. I could keep it in its place
even in spring,
walking my beat

over the charcoal lawns,
past the dun
forsythia, under
the cypresses, whose inky tips
scribbled in the wind.

I was not taken in
by the ripped arms waving
from a fence post—the last
intruder's jacket. His parachute
made beautiful sheets.

Nothing, nothing, nothing.
The birds and the snipers
were still in their nests;
the strafing planes
were resting their stiff wings.

I couldn't afford to rest.
I kept my hands
suspended, tense, over my hips, in case—
Suddenly a too-
specific rustle. I spun,

pistol cocked, and watched
a rabbit bound
between the strands
of barbed wire
into no-man's-land.

An owl rose
and flapped after it,
leaving a shuddering fir
and a single
languid quill

that detached itself
from the ruffled dark
and described an irregular
spiral, point-
first, into

my outstretched hand.
And as I reached
to grasp it, maybe I exposed
a sliver of white wrist.
Maybe I opened my mouth

and let my teeth catch
the starlight. I know my mind
wandered, just
for an instant, but
long enough. The shot

hissed into a puddle at my feet.
I froze.
My ears and nose
twitched: sulfur. What
had found its way behind my lines?

On my hands and knees,
I probed the mud
delicately.
Strange. The angle of entry
was nearly 90 degrees.

But overhead
were only early leaves,
still fuzzy and furled.
No solid perch, no cover for whoever
wanted me dead.

Early leaves and fading sky.
I knew better than to try
to focus too closely; my eyes played
as I had taught them, to either
side of what may

or may not have been there,
and, for an instant,
I thought I could see
a bulk too large, too motionless,
in the whipped canopy,

and then again, not.
This one was clever,
a master of surprise.
I wanted to meet him.
I wanted to hear the thud

of him hitting the ground
and smell his blood.
I wanted to tell his bones:
I will not tolerate
meddlers or spies!

I had infrared
sensors, and sensors
that could pick up the heat
of a living assassin crouched
invisible in lilacs.

My portable screen
would show him blinking
luminous green,
fixed in my sights—
plenty of time to aim.

But nothing of any size
was coming in. The heights
registered vacant, and now the massed
clouds were letting nothing else
in or out. My fire

would bring no one down.
Anyway, it was too late.
Already the dark was frayed,
curling to reveal
a margin of white,

and soon the ashen trees
would reignite
and blacken the grass with new
shadows. A light
mist was beginning to rise,

filling the space between
my enemy and me.
I felt a rhythmic disturbance, a pulse
like heavy wings withdrawing
into the gathering blue.

I couldn't suppress a smile.
I'd slipped, I admit,
but maybe it was just as well.
No showdown. Not quite yet.
I'd let the game go on a while,

let him—or her, or it—
underestimate me
while I refined
my methods and composed a more
inscrutable disguise.

Sooner or later, it would forget
itself, and show its hand.
Then I would get it right
between the eyes.
Another night.

Riverwards—Directives and Spells for Use in a Borderland

(suggested by Old English and Old High German magic spells, and by the landscape along the river Oder, the German-Polish border)

To Find a Certain Place

First you must decide which side   of the river you are on.
Language will not necessarily   signify. With so much
back and forth now, who knows   who speaks what where?

Most roads will be unmarked,   and you mustn't trust
the old men on benches   outside the Anglers' Rest.
They don't like strangers. They'll smile   and steer you wrong.

Watch where the sun sets.   You want the West
on your left, downstream,   where the river drains
sanguine towards the sea.   If you need to cross

you will have to arrange   that passage separately
and start again.   Wait until late
in the year and the day.   Then follow the water

into the fire, but keep your eye   on the opposite shore
where cannon-barrel chimneys are discharging   more gray
into the concrete sky   and the horizon closes like a sluice

between otherwise   identical elements.
Soon, as if by chance,   a silver Mercedes will sail by, not
going your way, its windows opaque   with the last of the light.

Squint, and mark   where the flashes from its chrome
bounce off the river at you.   When you see one catch
in a treetop, run—   it will be gone

by the time you arrive   but a black, resinous crust
may still be smoldering   down the trunk. Touch the largest root.
If your fingers burn,   you've found the spot: Dig here.

Against the Falling Sickness

When one falls   beside himself
in mid-stride or mid-sentence,   and flaps about
like a hooked trout,   his mouth
straining and snapping,   his lungs filled with flame,

draw across his chest   the river sign,
and speak these words: *Man of the earth,*
Satan is playing you in   on his long, strong line.
Whatever dainty bait   you have tasted, try

to spit it out.   Shake your head and rise
upright again, albeit   with bleeding lips.
Now take from his person   a button or a pin,
cast it into the coursing   stream, and say:

Father of all wrong,   this breathless soul, wriggling
between worlds, is not   worthy of your wiles.
Return him to his right   element to fatten, that you may
have more sport of him   another day.

FOR A BOUNTIFUL HARVEST

Maybe you crave   a banana. This is probably
too much to ask.   Imports are limited;
the stores in these parts   are generally empty, except
for a few wrinkled roots,   jars of syrupy fruit,
crates of beer, cigarettes,   and dusty bars of soap.

But if you've been living   for what feels like forever
on vacuum-packed bread   and canned goulash soup,
the first spring wind   sings to you of strawberries,
ramps, rhubarb, watercress,   sorrel, fiddleheads,
and the tender spears   old-timers call "sparrowgrass."

You walk past black fields,   imagining armies
of succulent shoots   about to pierce the surface.
You picture the barren trees   dripping cherries.
If you want a feast   in a few weeks, you must first
purchase the cooperation   of the elements.

Sharpen and clean   your pocketknife,
and on a night   when the moon is fat and freckled like a ripe
gooseberry, go   to where the river carves
its powerful furrow.   The moon will be admiring herself
splayed white on the stream,   fondled by ripples.

Appeal to her vanity, saying: *Delectable goddess,*
you are constantly consumed   by the insatiable dark,
yet you germinate anew   and grow plump again each month.
Encourage the sluggish   buds to swell to bountiful
fullness, like you.   Look, I will follow

the river's example and feed   the winter-parched earth
with a little of my life.   Now cut a fingertip and squeeze out three
big red pips: one each for river, earth, and moon.
If they are pleased, the lazy pulse   of the cold land will quicken,
and soon the musty shops   will be transformed, perfumed

with savory and mint. By June,   fruit will be falling so fast
you can't keep up; you'll fill   basket after oozing basket
then collapse in the shade   to watch the air writhing in the heat
and yellow jackets   marching daintily across
pink heaps of peaches   in search of sugary wounds.

INTERDICTION

It is forbidden   to set your hair on fire,
to tie knots   in a dead man's belt or pound his chest
with carding combs.   There are therapists
and other legitimate   professionals to help you. Invest
in bonds. Stop   trying to divine where pots

of gold lie buried   in other folks' backyards.
You con men who claim   to see the future in the scratches
of a fat corn-fed cock,   or the rough brushstrokes
of windblown branches   across the sky,
remember your fellow conjurers   behind bars.

All their auguries   didn't get them far.
The harsh penalties   for peddling hope
are for your own protection;   it is foolish to poke
your clumsy fingers   into the thin
membrane between   us and what's beyond.

Let the dead alone.   Wash your tea leaves
down the drain.   Don't disturb the dryads
asleep in their trees   or the nixies resting
in their waterbeds.   You think it sounds
like an interesting challenge   to try to unbend

the river by speaking spells   over a snakeskin?
Think again.   When the water wants
to change its course,   no words of yours
will sway it either way.   Worse, you may anger
forces more merciless   than civil law.

Desist, therefore,   from fretting the unseen powers,
lest some weary spirit,   molested once too often
with frivolous petitions,   should sweep you
off the slippery riverbank into   the rapidly
departing stream with one impatient   swipe of his paw.

LOVE CHARM

Choose the right moon: not too full
if the beloved is small;   sharp horns if he or she
is already another's.   Gather twenty-eight
leaves of linden or beech   in a rush basket, lined
with fine blue cloth.   In fine blue ink,

inscribe one leaf   with the beloved's name. Repeat
each night until   the same moon returns,
then go to the river,   choosing a place
where it runs deep and fast;   scatter
the leaves across the water,   saying, as they whirl away:

For you [name] I hold   my breath. For you my head
spins, and my heart   races out of control,
light as these leaves.   And as the passionate rapids
wrap around my flanks,   so may you, too,
embrace me soon.   Now jump, clothes and all.

You must go in over your head,   or the charm will not take.
Your shirt should fall   up under your armpits
and your hair should wave   above you like the foliage
of an underwater tree.   The longer you stay down,
the stronger the spell.   By the time you pull yourself,

panting, back onto the bank,   the beloved, asleep
under a blue blanket,   will already feel
the current stirring, will reach   eagerly out, almost awake,
as if to grasp at something floating past,   then sink
into a deeper, clearer dream: your face

drifting pale but indelible   among moonlit reeds.
All night, while the blue ink bleeds   into the blue stream,
the beloved will be slowly suffused   with desire for you,
and at first dawn   will rush headlong across drenched lawns
into your arms, as the names   swirl into the sea.

To Be Rid of a Rival

For this curse,   you need a liter of good grain liquor
and a heartful   of unquenchable hate.
Keep the bottle corked,   and spend a long, dry night
thinking of everything   your rival has
that ought to be yours.   At dawn, roll up your trousers

and set off barefoot   down an unmaintained
side road that dissolves into sand,   then dead-ends
at the river.   Walk upstream until you see
the swift skein of the water   tangle and fray,
marking the snag   where the river dumps its garbage.

An almost spokeless   bicycle wheel, an oil drum,
two traffic cones,   and the aluminum
bones of a beach chair   have fetched up on this altar
of wet rock and weed.   Wade in as close
as you can to make your own   ugly offering.

The stream may be icy,   but your stoked-up rage
will keep you warm   as you unstop the bottle
and drink deep,   wishing your rival
gone gone gone gone.   Your curse will gain
strength with every swig.   Picture a heart attack;

picture a jittery   mugger with a gun;
a missed stoplight   and a truck; a sailboat
in a thunderstorm.   When your head starts to swim,
take a final pull   then throw the bottle hard
onto the trash heap. A trail   of white lightning will

glitter for an instant like shards   of glass across the air.
Wish once more.   If your libation is accepted,
some misfortune will soon   carry your rival off—
cast away, washed up—   until nothing is left
but a slight catch   in the river's throat.

For One Troubled by Internal Pain

If you awake   from dark dreams, attacked
by an inner ache;   if night after night,
you lie breathless and sweating   with the great effort
of waiting for the pain to fade,   and your days are dizzy
from loss of sleep;   if your doctor can discover

no other evidence   of infection, and the X-rays show
everything intact,   but still some greedy shade
seems to be feeding   amidst the voluptuous
blood-stuffed bags   and tender undulations
of your gut,   you must propitiate the incubus thus:

take at least a pound   of good lean lamb or beef
seasoned with salt and juniper,   and a full flask
of ruby port.   Walk to where the willows slump
over the riverbank, and the black   soil is tender, swollen
with warm rot.   Dig there as deep

as your arm can reach,   lay your offering down,
and with one hand   touching your own
afflicted part,   say: *Dirty spirit, cramped*
in inadequate quarters,   this richly furnished new
hole is for you.   May your tongue and teeth

delight in such soft   unrepentant meat,
and may you smile   on the multitudes
of earwigs and worms   already burrowing up
to serve you—so much more   agreeable than this, your poor
ill-appointed host.   Now, quickly, the wine.

Shake out every drop   and before it sinks in
take yourself home, but note: For three days you must eat

only stone fruit: plums,   peaches, and the like, whose sweet
dripping flesh conceals   a heart hard enough
to crack the cruel   tooth of any trouble.

To Dispatch a Restless Spirit

Sometimes the body departs this world   but the spirit
digs in its heels, unwilling   to leave its old home.
It becomes a nuisance,   refusing to budge
from its former chair   or let guests use its favorite cup.

Do not upset it further   by calling in a priest.
Take a positive approach,   portraying passing
as a step up,   stressing the advantages
of severing ties to the far inferior   material realm.

Early in the morning, coax the ghost   out of the house
and down the overgrown   towpath. The air
above the invisible river   should still be swarming
with pearly fog.   Point out the landmarks

that are no longer there: the old grist mill
replaced by tall gray housing blocks,   the jagged stumps
of what used to be a bridge,   the family of ducks
paddling near the spot   where a border guard

once shot a swimmer.   Remind it how eager
most souls are to leave: *Do you see any phantom horses
towing spectral barges?   Of course not. They cast off
their earthly traces first   chance they got, to gallop*

away and roll in celestial clover   on the distant shore.

Even the morning mist   is rushing up to meet the rising sun
and burn itself to pure,   blissful bodilessness.
Don't listen to those   scaredy-cats the shadows,

who never get above the ground—   you deserve more!
While the spirit peers   tentatively into
the glowing void,   turn and tiptoe home. With luck,
it will decide to cross over   and stay put. But

just in case, sprinkle your lintels   with river water,
and for at least a week   keep the windows shut
and wear earplugs to sleep,   so you won't have to hear
if a diaphanous fist   comes pounding on the door.

To Cross Safely over Thin Ice

This spell is not recommended.   Although it looks simple,
it is difficult to execute correctly   and the risk is great.
Far better to wait   until the ice has washed away, then pay
for the necessary documents   and take the ferry.

If you insist   on indulging your restlessness
and ignoring the *DANGER!* signs,   be sure to assuage
the disapproving spirits   by demonstrating
your humility.   Leave your heavy overcoat

and boots at home.   Wear old clothes, and carry
only what will fit   into the smallest daypack.
With each excess   ounce, your chances
of success decrease.   Approach the thin-skinned river

on your hands and knees,   whispering an Our Father

and earnest entreaties   to whatever other, earthier
deities might be   crouching behind a black-speckled snowbank
or peering between the planks   of a rotting flatboat.

Don't raise your voice.   Don't raise your head.
Inch across the ice   on your belly, propelling yourself
by twisting your hips   and casting out your hands
to latch on to any possibly stable   irregularity:

flotsam frozen in place   or fissures
you hope won't expand.   Dig in your nails
and pull. Your forehead must   touch the ice crust
and you must say *Please*   and *Thank you* for each tiny

uncatastrophic advance.   By midstream,
your pelvis will be bruised,   your fingers swollen almost double
their proper size, the dripping tip   of your red nose
white with frostbite.   If your performance

amuses those   who dictate whether or not
the surface will hold,   you may make it all the way across
and haul yourself, stiff   and filthy, up onto a shore
indistinguishable   from the one you left.

Don't let your guard down yet;   you'll hear a crack
like a rifle shot.   This could be the river warning you
you can't go back,   or it could be the sky
expressing its displeasure   in out-of-season thunder.

Run for cover before   the lowering clouds collapse under
their own weight, and hail   comes rattling down
in sharp metallic shards   like shrapnel, or
big gray chunks like the rubble   of an exploded bunker.

To Leave a Place of Ill Luck

This spell will work   only in early spring.
Have ready: a small balsawood   or plastic plane—
the type propelled by a tightly   twisted rubber band.

Monitor the iced-over river;   the morning
after it cracks,   stand on the bank
facing east,   with the plane in your hand,

and speak to each   winter-weary element
in turn, beginning: *Unlucky land,*
maybe the frost heaves   have finally

shaken out the rocks   that blocked last year's harvest.
I wish you the best,   but let us both start
over again, apart.   Hard river, stuck

for months in this one blighted spot,   the sun is back
to turn you loose at last.   I know you're aching
to be on the move.   I'm ready, too.

Watch me escape!   Now hold up
your plane, making sure   the motor is wound
almost to the breaking point.   Ignore the river's laughter;

it will never understand   the principle of flight.
Turn to the sky, and say: *Pale sun, come closer,*
unlock   the soil around my roots.

Push the river faster through   its sluices and quicken
the earthbound breeze   so it will carry me
to an easier place.   And you, heavy air,

wake up! Blow the coal smoke   over the border.
It's time to breathe in   a sweeter, lighter season.
I hereby entrust this little   vessel to your care.

Please lift its wings.   With these words, release
your airship in whatever   direction the wind
is taking that day.   Some will tell you the success

of your spell depends   on where the plane alights.
This is not true.   If you have invoked
the elements correctly,   the very act

of letting it go   guarantees that your own
tensely coiled inner   spring will leap open
and set you happily   adrift again.

Whiz Mob

(based on David W. Maurer's 1955 Whiz Mob: A Correlation
of the Technical Argot of Pickpockets with Their Behavior
Pattern*)*

ON THE WHIZ

The mark has to be
moving, so the touch will feel
like part of himself.

A crush helps. The more
chumps, the more chance of a clean
anonymous score.

We work the get-ons,
the rattlers, and the third rail,
where the tips are thick.

Forget casinos.
Tracks, too. You don't have a prayer.
They're wall-to-wall pinks.

A hook develops
a nose for a well-lined poke.
Threads don't signify.

Even a rufus
might have a fat ox tongue full
of soft on his prat.

Fingers you can train,
guts you can build, but you're born
with grift sense, or not.

Can you move a mark
without him knowing? You might
make a bang-up wire.

SAFETY MEASURES

First, get off the nut.
This will cost a bundle, but
then you own the line.

If a local put
the X on a certain spot,
lay off it, or else.

For every tool, top
priority goes to not
rumbling the come-on.

Careful mechanics
know when to stop. There's always
other okuses.

Keep yourself clean. Cut
the scores up regularly,
and ding the dead ones.

Stick with the class guns.
Pickups got an awful name
for burning touches.

Most good mobs won't hold
on to paper. Not even
whiskers stiffs—just scratch.

When you're in the hall
of fame, watch out for whiz dicks
with camera eyes.

Take along a sheet
to shade your dukes, and never
give up your kisser.

READ YOUR MARK

Without you can read
your mark, fast fingers don't count
for diddly-squat.

That cousin looks soft.
Anything in his britches?
Maybe; maybe not.

Is he even on
the level? You learn to smell
a plant a mile off.

A walk that don't match
the threads, a wad of cush flashed
too obviously.

If you interpret
the mark correctly, he'll lead
you straight to his hide.

A man's poke talks with
his hand. Nervous patting says:
I'm here and I'm fat.

Your mark may be thick,
but his hindside knows what's what,
and it doesn't lie.

He shifts. He twitches.
His kiester is suspicious,
ripe for a rumble.

That's your cue to let
go the score before his prat
wises up his head.

THE FRAME

You've spotted your mark.
You office your stall, cut in,
and the frame closes.

A sensitive stall
picks up on a cannon's plan
automatically.

He'll turn the sucker
into you, and stick him there
while you make your play.

Jostling's a myth.
Jostle the mark, and he'll round
and beef gun for sure.

No class mob resorts
much to the rowdy-dowdy.
Long-term, it won't pay.

The frame should be tight
but flexible; you work with
what the mark gives you.

He walks, you walk—smooth
and natural-like. He's beat,
but he don't savvy.

It happens his arms
are momentarily not
at his disposal.

That's your front man's back
he's facing. Now you're ready
to locate his hide.

Is there a wad worth
forking on this egg? You reach
in the frame to see.

HOW TO LOCATE

The chump's in your lap,
your stall's throwing up a hump,
and the score's waiting.

Run your shaded dukes
over the mark until you
find the impression.

Fan his sacks, his pits,
his bridges, his plants. The book
could be anywhere.

Scratch, leather, or both?
A cordeen? A tweezer poke?
Your fingers can tell.

You might feel a thick
skin riding conveniently
high, ready to pop.

Or maybe that bump
on the hip's a roll of rag
right in a tog tail.

It'll mean more work
if he's got his nipple nailed
in his insider.

Once you know where what
you want is, you can address
yourself to the kick.

SIZING UP THE KICK

You locate. Let's say
left britch. Nothing to unslough.
Now, how does it lay?

An educated
guess can save a dip a lot
of unpleasantness.

A sock on its feet,
nice and loose, gives you a shot
at a quick kick out.

When the skin's on edge
or laying down is harder.
You can't just spear it.

Top hooks take one look
at a chump and know just how
his britches will play.

Watch the wrinkles. They
show how the material
will act in your hand.

Fabric, cut, load, fit,
oil from the skin—everyone's
kicks is different.

Some kicks reef up fast—
finger and thumb—one good tug,
and the scratch will spring.

Extra resistance,
extra force. Stiff kicks need less
delicate tactics.

With a handle on
the properties of the kick,
you're ready to swing.

THE TOUCH

Readjust the frame.
Make sure there's no law in sight.
Synchronize rhythms.

You're on. Performance
time: ten seconds, tops, and no
audience, you hope.

Everything looks like
nothing—just you and the chump
moving together.

Casual elbows
keep him from checking a slight
tickle in his kick.

All your fingers do
is persuade the fabric to
deliver the score.

You work it up and
work it up; top it up. Now
you own it—it's off!

No time to turn it
over yet. You'll meet and ding
the leathers later.

Duke it to your stall.
He cops, and the sucker still
don't know he's been stuck.

You're back in the push,
far from the mark, by the time
he tumbles and blows.

Family Outfit

My old man was just
a carnival cootie but
he turned me out fine.

He kept us in threads
and never got tangled up
in heavier rackets.

Almost as soon as
I could walk, I was stalling
for Pop in the traps.

My favorite spots
were canvas operas, pit
shows, and five-in-ones.

When a line got hot,
we'd lay dead a spell or light
out for the rat stop.

Kinky kayducers
were Pop's best friends. We'd hopscotch
for months for peanuts.

Twelve years on the boost—
from Cisco to Chi, we trimmed
hotels and hoosiers.

Moll-buzzing season
was around the holidays,
when hangers were fat.

It ended when Pop
got guzzled in a pea soup
tip at the rag top.

Even though he copped,
they settled him with a full
sixer in the can.

Our tribe was broke up.
I nailed the next rattler and
struck out one-handed.

ETHICS

The mob has its code.
Never wise up a sucker.
Buy hot. Keep the meet.

Standard excuses
for missing a meet: the three
S's—shit, shave, shine.

No one clips against
his principles. Certain guns
won't nail certain marks.

We respect it when
a pious cannon declares
himself out on priests.

In with the grief, in
with the gravy. Cough up your
fall dough, split the score.

We'll go for a dip
that's down or in the can, up
to a couple C's.

None of the rackets
knock each other, and of course
nobody peaches.

Always, everywhere,
we office at the slightest
suspicion of fur.

THE FIX AND THE FALL

The fuzz knows the whiz
and vice versa. This leads to
cooperation.

Your average dick
is on the shake. A little
jack will make him right.

Count on a C-note
per man per day; if there's no
bad beefs, you're OK.

Once you've fixed the bull,
even when a mark blows, he'll
give you a pass-up.

Fit the fur the best
you can, but an airtight fix
is impossible.

We've all had bad falls:
the rapper won't stop yelling,
and the sham won't take.

He makes the sneeze. What's
next depends on how much scratch
you have in your seams.

Even if you're caught
dead to rights, with fall dough up
you'll stay out of stir.

No mob wants its hook
in the bucket, so they'll grind
up nickels and dimes.

Everyone's happy.
The button is squared, for now,
and the wire is sprung.

CURDLED FIX

You can hooverize
on rags or grub, but you can't
skinch on the grease job.

Down in the Cap once,
my troupe of top mechanics
flopped on a bad fix.

We thought we were right—
the usual shake artists,
the usual shade.

It turned out our brains
got a cramp in his hands, and
hadn't fixed the flat.

Or maybe Paddy
did us dirty, or our rod
stuck to the ointment.

We were in the chutes,
batting away, when socko!
Fur was everywhere.

Okay, we were made.
Was there any way to stay
in circulation?

Tried slipping the blue
a fin, a saw, two bits. He
was untouchable.

We called our doctor.
We called our best safety pin.
No one could bounce us.

After our hitches,
you bet we up and dusted!
That burg was hoodooed.

KNOCKABOUT

I was on the outs.
C.O.D. I even sunk
to hustling the flops.

At a sinker shop,
a mission stiff put me wise
to a makeshift mob.

It was a punk troupe:
jam-snatchers, rollers, bookmen,
and summertime tools.

Zero class, but all
right by me. I was hungry
and they filled me in.

Our line was frisking
plus a little pocket-prowl,
and of course the boost.

We could pull enough
junker touches to keep off
the belly-wrinkles.

If we hit a flush,
we'd find some forty-fours, or
score some heaven dust.

Then a psalm singer
bum-fingered us on an old
elevation job.

The buzz was, the brass
had us clocked. They were ready
to send us to school.

I got the needles.
I didn't feature myself
in numbers again.

When I seen a D
shepherding me, I amscrayed,
and that's all she wrote.

CLOSE CALL

They say a winner
never wears the gloves, but how
about the bracelets?

One time, I admit,
I played center field myself
and ducked a wallop.

I was on the dodge
and sneeze-shy—thought every bates
was a fuzzy-tail.

It was a speedfest,
a three-handed pickup mob
with me on backstop.

Mick catches a fat
flash. Frenchy gets his hump up,
but my moxie's low.

Then I spot the arm
giving us the double-O
by the payoff pole.

Mick's already throwed
his mitt. I step back. Too late
to office "Elbow!"

Flatty hasn't pegged
me yet, so I knock a fast
fade into the squeeze.

Here comes the button
on the highball. His wood's out.
The score hits the floor.

My boys are dropping.
I see the hoops, and take it
on the heel and toe.

TEAM

That fall I was down
on my luck, fresh from the joint,
muzzling in the sheds.

One mark I couldn't
budge. I like to broke a leg
trying to prat him out.

When I felt a hand
around mine, I thought for sure
it was Richard Dick.

That mark was a tool!
We neither of us knew how
we'd missed the other.

Didn't I feel fine
sitting in a goulash house
punching gun again!

We figured why not
play it two-handed? We hit
the chutes and cleaned up.

We'd move through a push
racking up so many pokes
our own kicks were stuffed.

Right spots or hot spots,
we rooted in, always on
the drag together.

I guess our heads got
swelled. We turned brassy and walked
into a collar.

He was hooking, so
they clawed him. I took leg bail
and dusted my tail.

CLASS TIP

The classiest tip
I ever worked was a show
at intermission.

All the eggs had gold
props in their chokers, and silk
even for their wipes.

Plenty of onions,
plenty of rope. Some of it
was just shag, of course.

I was done up sharp.
Duds like that, wouldn't no one
pin me for a dip.

A glass of bubbly
in one hand, the other in
the britches for skins.

Naturally swells
got protection. Everywhere
you looked was the eye.

Watched a pink not see
me and my stalls frame and clip
a dozen fat marks.

Just for fun, I asked
one dumb bull the time, then banged
his souper and slang.

By the bell, I'd slipped
my duke-man over three G's,
real gentlemanly.

Beg your pardon, sir,
but I believe your britch kick
just lost its leather.

SINGLE O TOOL

I got me a name.
That meant I could write my own
ducket anywhere.

Filled in here, filled in
there. But a live wire gets tired
of splitting his score.

Working single o,
I don't have to be no one
else's producer.

No meets to make, no
backstop, no front man, no steer—
I'm my own whole mob.

Instead of a stall,
I can use a fat lady's
prat to shade my dukes.

Lonesome? A little.
But now I hold on to all
my touches myself.

Even over and
above the nut, I still knock
up more than before.

I could fit a swell
skirt out in the slickest skins,
cover her with stones.

Had a lapful once,
but she took a powder when
she heard I was whiz.

Twists

A twist on the whiz
gets her cut of the knock-up
like anyone else.

In a tip, a frail
can get away with more, so
moll mobs root right in.

Suckers worrying
about their pokes don't expect
a pinch from a twist.

With their tiny mitts,
skirts can reach inside a britch
and fish out the skin.

Broads plant their kiesters
under a chump to keep his
mind off his own prat.

For a sharp twist, life
on the grift usually beats
going on the turf.

Sometimes she's saddled
with a middle britch tool who
takes most of her end.

When he's biting butts,
a cannon might send his moll
on the boost or worse.

This one gun, his gal
hustled for years to keep him,
Chinaman and all.

But when he got kissed
by a mob, he blowed her off
for some other twist.

HOLE-UP

Every fingersmith
needs a drum where he can play
possum for a spell.

Say there's a reader
out on you, and your choirboy
is about to spill.

One more flop, and you'll
be doing the book. It's time
to go on the hush.

With a good inkpot,
you can just rabbit it off,
and bingo—you're low.

Fit your layoff spot
with a kiester full of cush
and a soft crumb-box.

Get a solid stooge
to see to the these and those,
the chuck and the slush.

Now you're on the plush.
Unkink. Leave the ragged edge
to the whistle man.

My hole in the hub
was grade-A cream—even had
a noisiola.

I'd invite my best
twist, and we'd make my diggings
a red-hot mushroom.

That was one sweet cave.
Sometimes I wished I could stay
dead there forever.

PIPEFEST

Ran into Murphy
at a gallop and we had
a good long chow-round.

He gave me the noise
on buzzards I'd grifted with
donkey's years ago.

It's sad. Even ace
friskers wind up poppyheads
or pimples or crumbs.

Just one in gravy:
Frenchy learned green goods and got
stinking on sour dough.

Marco, who was so
slick with the heavy lard, went
into the bunko.

Art got plugged. Masher
is macking, like you'd expect
from such a gash-hound.

That boiled dinner Spuds,
who belched on me in Beantown,
is inside himself.

Corky's little nag
made him quit the whiz, and now
he's a kosher slave.

The real staggerer
was Jock: seems some burned-up mark
crunched both his lunch-hooks.

His forks aren't up to
digging, so he's wiped his nose
and bleats for the bulls.

I couldn't hardly
swallow that, but Murph is George,
so I guess it goes.

The Whiz Is Dying

The whiz is dying.
Seems like no one's interested
in nailing a hide.

All the class cannons
have passed, and the kids don't have
no grift know no more.

How long has it been
since I seen a sucker in
an elegant frame?

What whiz there is is
crapper hustlers, lush busters—
strictly root and toot.

Imagine a stall
can't raust, can't stick, don't even
know the offices.

Nowadays coppers
are mostly wrong, and the best
old lines are burned up.

Sure, there's lots of tips,
but without a single dip
getting his mitt down.

Tuesday afternoons,
me and some other wires meet,
cut up old touches.

We watch the pushes
on the stems and in the sheds—
nothing but slave grift.

The action's gone. Soon
you won't find one gun can still
spin the whiz lingo.

Pinocchio—The <u>Real</u> Story!

*Exclusive Interviews with the First Puppet
to Star in His Own Hollywood Biopic!*

*Featuring: Shocking Revelations—How the Novel and
the Movie Got It Wrong!*

*Intimate Secrets—What They Didn't Want
You to Know About Jiminy Cricket!*

*Authentic Flashbacks—Life Behind the
Scenes at Disney Studios!*

PINOCCHIO REMEMBERS THE TOY SHOP

Did I run out on the guy that made me?   Sure.
I'm not denying that, but   listen, there's
two sides to every story.   Here's me—young,
not bad-looking, smart, ambitious—   cooped up
in a toy shop with a nut   who gets his kicks
jerking me around on strings!

                                    "Kindly, smiling
old Geppetto!"—   the press sells you the standard
line of paternalistic   propaganda;
they always use   that picture where he's staring
at my empty place,   and his cheeks are streaked
with big, well-lit tears.   Why? Because he'd lost
his most promising slave!

                            You want to hear
the real scoop?   Talk to the Jack-in-the-Box.
He'll tell you a thing or two   about our poor
forsaken father.   No one ever knew
what Jack had done   to get himself locked down.
We all cringed   when we heard that tune begin—
Round and round

the cobbler's bench, the monkey
chased the weasel—   saw the old man cranking away,
held our breath   waiting for the *Pop!* when Jack
would explode from his hole.   He'd meet our eyes
as he hurled his heavy   head from side to side
and flailed his stunted arms,   convulsing
at the end of his spring.

                    We couldn't move
our mouths, of course, so we kept   smiling at his
manic rictus, until   he got slammed back
into solitary.   *"'Twas all in fun."* Like hell!
That man was sick!   Nowadays, somebody
would turn him in,   but this was way back when,
in the old country.

                    Then there were the cuckoo clocks—
dozens of them!   Imagine all the pendulums,
not even in synch,   swinging every which way,
as if the walls   were full of hypnotists.
Tick tock tick tock—all day, all night.   *You* try
to sleep or think!   And just when you've almost
blocked it out? That's right:

                    Cuckoo! The locks click:
It's exercise time!   Each Swiss precision-
engineered prison   stages its hourly
public reenactment   of some old crime
or punishment: The father methodically
paddles his bad child;   the farmer chases
the hysterical

                    turkey in circles;
the drunk with his derby   askew, wobbles
around his lamppost;   six identical
cancan girls   flip up their skirts, presenting
their lovingly painted rumps;   a soldier
blasts another soldier.   Can you blame me

for lighting out first chance I got?

                                Besides,
you have to wonder.   Maybe he had the last
laugh after all.   I made it big—OK,
but sometimes everything   seems just the same:
the klieg lights   like interrogators' lamps,
the kicking chorus line—   *Hold those smiles!*—
of marionette Rockettes,

                            the maestro's
metronome   tick-tocking as I run through
my big number ("No Strings")   again and again
and again, dead beat,   dripping (I'm real now!) sweat,
aching in every hollow bone,   my flimsy
cartilaginous   connective tissues
wearing thin,

                      and no one to repair them.
I'll bet you even this   was part of his plan.
They want real! I'll give 'em real!   *Cut 'em loose, and—*
out of the frying pan   into real fire.
I bet that kindly, smiling   s.o.b.'s
still there, behind the scenes,   watching us dance
ourselves into the ground,   rubbing his big hands.

Flashback: Pinocchio's Makeover

WANT TO BE REAL?   CERTIFIED PROFESSIONAL
SELF-ACTUALIZATION   TRAINER WILL
MAKE YOUR DREAM COME TRUE!   *Oh, yes! Teach me how*
to do what people do!   *I'm positive*
I've got what it takes,   *if only I could*
stop being wood.
                      Wood? I'm afraid that poses
additional difficulties....   *Please! Look!*

I've got looks, I've got charm, I've got smarts,   I've got
the check all written out!   Hmmm.... Let me see.
Come closer. Maybe, maybe....   Yes! You're rough,
terribly rough, of course   (a textbook case
of splinters—and those knots!),

                              but underneath
I think I can detect   a glimmer of
Star Quality.   *Thank you! I always knew*
that someday someone....   Mind you, I can't make
any guarantees   (your signature here, please,
and here, and here)—   *No, no—I just need*
a little polish, a few

                    connections and
a tip or two   on the tricks of the trade—
like how to move   my eyes and mouth so people
will believe,   or what they mean when they talk
about their brains and hearts.   I got your name
from the Tin Woodsman.   He said you set him up
with his big break.

                    Ah yes, he did nicely
once we worked the rust   out of his system.
But you have to understand,   reinventing
your personal dynamic   may entail
sacrifices. *Anything!*   Well, let's start
with those dreadful strings.   Don't you feel how they're
tying you down?

                    They are? I always thought
they were holding me up.   Oh dear, that shows
how deep the problem goes.   You've internalized
energy-draining   body-negative
patterns of self-denial.   Our twelve-week
introductory course   in body-mind
attitudinal alignment,

                    taught by top

empowerment counselor,   Dr. Désirée
Newman, Ph.D.   (one session free
if you register today)   will help you
give yourself permission   to pursue
your wildest dreams.   *Will I learn how to smile
and sweat and blush and bleed?*

Naturally!
"Strength Through Joy"   is our most popular workshop.
You'll laugh, you'll cry, you'll finally   let down your hair!
I can't—it's painted on.   That was only
a figure of speech;   you're going to have to try
not to be so literal.   But now
that you mention it,

of course you'll also want
some facial enhancement.   Our stylists
are geniuses with   sandpaper and chisels.
They'll shave the gnarly grain   off your cheeks
and do something about   that unfortunate nose.
Will it hurt?   Most of our clients do report
some discomfort, yes;

that's part of the process.
Remember, without wounds,   you'll never heal.
We use advanced   FDA-approved solvents
to break through   your defensive cellulose shell.
But if you think a slight   burning sensation
is too high a price   for releasing your inner
real boy, just say so, and—

No, no! Go on!
When the bandages come off   you'll have soft
supple lips to kiss   or pout or pronounce
Continental vowels.   Your eyes will be moist
and your pupils   will dilate extra-wide
for that big box-office   Bambi-anime
vulnerability.

And will I really be
real?   You'll be so real you won't believe it!
People on the street   will say, "Look at that boy!
He's the real thing, no question!"   Those holes
in your hands and feet   will close. No more broken
promises, no more lies   once you're in control
of your own destiny.

                    I'm ready! Fine.
Lean back, get comfortable,   and we'll begin.
Visualize   your new, real self. I'll just
slip these little   security bands around
your ankles and wrists   to help you maintain
total relaxation.   OK—you may feel
a tiny pinch now   as the needle goes in.

PINOCCHIO ON PROFESSIONAL RIVALRY

The trade rags   had it right, for once, about
me and the cricket;   we never got along.
God knows I tried!   When casting sent over
this pip-squeak from Hicksville   to be my sidekick,
I knocked myself out   showing him the ropes.
Big mistake!

                    Next thing I know, this so-called
"conscience," this   glory-grabbing humbug, is
stealing every scene,   reading *me* the rules!
A bug! Not that I got   anything against
insects, but you know what I mean.   That part
started out tiny—   a dozen lines, tops,
then sayonara.

                    In the book, I took
him out with a mallet   in chapter four.
(A boffo bit!   Too bad it got the scissors!)

He didn't even have a name,   never mind
second billing and   the opening song.
But the front room figured   the Holy Joe
angle would play

              in Peoria, so
they duded him up: cut off a couple of legs,
covered the antennae   with a stovepipe hat,
gave him an umbrella,   a morning coat,
a cutesy moniker   (*Jiminy?* Jesus!),
and a custom-made set   of fingers to wag
in yours truly's face.

            And did he go for it?
You should have seen   that sorry old knockabout
in his go-to-meeting clothes,   shimmying
with the music-box chorines.   By week two
he's sneaking up to rewrite   with "a few
little ideas,"   all of which, of course,
involve more lines for him.

            Excuse me, *who's*
the headliner here?   Where was he before
this gig made him legit?   Playing haylofts
in jerkwater towns.   Now he's an expert!
Now he's everywhere,   cracking wise, taking pratfalls—
what he calls   "comic relief"—what *I* call
murdering the script.

            Collodi's concept
was solid gold: a poor, motherless boy,
naïve but warmhearted,   pluckily pursues
his dream: He's tired   of being just a toy;
he wants to be *real.*   There's Oedipal tension, too,
so he sets off, brave and bold,   only to learn
how cruel the real world can be.

            He's swindled!
Robbed! Jailed! Beaten! Sold   into slavery!

In spite of his handicaps   (wood, nose, strings),
our hero struggles onward,   saves his father's life,
and feels the first tender stirrings   of young love—
strictly class, no smut!   We could have been the next
David Copperfield!

                      But what hit the screens?
Cheap gags, slapstick,   and bimbos galore.
Even the goldfish   got tarted up! With no
legs or hips, she still   managed to sashay
around her bowl,   batting those extra-thick
Maybelline lashes   and making kissy-face
against the glass.

                    And don't get me started
on the ending.   Screenwriting 101:
You've followed the hero   through hair-raising chases,
kidnapping, swordplay, escape   from a moving whale!
Great stuff—but action alone   won't carry the show.
When it comes to the closer,   take it slow,
milk it for all it's worth.

                        Zoom in, tight shot
as he savors his bittersweet   coming-of-age
and delivers his big speech   about what it means
to be real. A genuine   tear catches
the bright reflection   of the wishing-star
on his soft, human cheek.   The orchestra swells—
and fade-out.... *The End.*

                      The suckers are wringing
their hankies, and sales   are through the roof. That's how
it *should* have been.   That's how it *was*, until
Judas Cricket   fast-talked the scriptists
into lowering the brow.   Stale cornpone
instead of catharsis,   dramatic unity
shot all to hell.

                When I saw the final cut

I called my lawyer, but   he said without
a veto clause, my hands were tied.   Not that I care
so much for myself;   it's a matter
of artistic principle.   Where's the logic?
I risk my ass   dragging the old man
back to dry land,

and apart from turning
into flesh and blood,   what thanks do I get?
Bupkes! The bug,   who's done nothing but kibitz,
gets an engraved eighteen-caret badge   ("Lord High
Keeper of the Knowledge of Right and Wrong"   my eye!),
a smooch   from the Blue Fairy, and a reprise
of his schlocky song,

then damned if the camera
doesn't follow   that dandified roach
right out the window   into the sunset,
leaving *me*   (the hero, remember?) back
on the toy-shop shelf,   and my climactic
existential soliloquy—   my ticket
to the Academy—   on the cutting-room floor.

PINOCCHIO'S PLEASURES

Playland? Oh, please!   Collodi bowdlerized
that episode but good!   Cotton candy,
wooden horses, jump ropes, clowns,   ring-around-
the-rosy? No way.   Disney understood
where you go when you ditch school: Pleasure Island.
Tobacco Road! Saloons!

We had times,
Lampwick and me, shooting craps,   shooting pool,
shooting the sitting-duck   shot glasses off
the bar until   the donkey fever hit.

And it was worth it.   Got that wise-ass cricket
lined up behind   the eight ball—then, whack!
Into a side pocket.
                          Handsome, handsome
in the frosty mirrors—   maraschino
cherries on every lip.   Effervescent
haloes buzzed   over our small, pink, hairless
human ears.   A troop of silver-tipped
bottles (at your service, sirs!)   bowed deep, jingling
the golden chains
                              around their empty necks.
But the houses were the best!   Locked closets
begging to be bashed open,   saucers dying
to fly.   It was curtains for the curtains,
and you should have seen me stomp   the Lemon Pledged
coffee tables.   Think I'm sentimental
about wood?
                    Well, I'm not. It reminds me
of everything I hate   about myself:
uncomfortable, stiff,   most of our future
whittled away, and, worst,   identifying
Stockholm syndrome–style   with the bastards
that carved us up.   Take the sanctimonious
bookcases, for example—
                              always so
fucking upright! Shelves   always parallel!
Lampwick and me, we   cut them down to size.
Then the hoity-toity   Chippendale side chairs
got theirs.   And finally (I cannot tell
a lie) with my little   ax, I hacked
the master bed
                    to smithereens and slept.
My splitting head   woke me up early.
The cheek on the pillow   beside me was gray.

Too many bristles.   I reached for my face
but my fingers weren't working.   His eyes
opened and rolled, panicky white.   We both
pulled our lips back   and began to bray.

FLASHBACK: PINOCCHIO LEARNS THE METHOD

Here's the deal: Your beloved father figure
has been swallowed by a whale.   Naturally
you're out to save him,   but right now you're stuck
on a sharp, slippery rock.   You've got ocean
pounding all around you—   how do you feel?
Uncomfortable? Cold?
                              Well, that's a start,
but you've got to take it deeper.   Come on,
you're helpless, alone,   the sunstruck sea
is flashing like knives   (that's Homer—remember,
a little poetry   classes up your act).
How about it?   It's pretty. It reminds me
of pictures.
                    No, no, no. Something from the gut!
Think shipwreck, fathomless   abyss, the awful,
awesome power   of nature, next to which
mankind is but—I see a fish.   OK.
We can work with that: the teeming life-force
glittering even in   the Stygian
bathysmal depths!
                          You wanted to be real—
am I right? So,   first step: let yourself go.
Unlock   your wooden chest and find a knot
to call a heart.   What's in it? Termites, rot.
No. Try again.   Remember the good old days

in the toy shop—the cozy glow   of the hearth,
you and Geppetto together....
                                        I hurt
where he drilled holes   and strung me through with wires
to make me move.   Excellent! Now channel
that anger and pain!   Look—here comes Monstro,
also known (taDUM!)   as "Leviathan,
crooked serpent,"   evil incarnate,
big as a city block!
                              Like the Good Book
says, you can't snag this one   with your little hook.
You've got to take the plunge!   *But I can't swim.*
Stop thinking negative;   you're a natural
flotation device.   Reach out and latch
on to that lip   even though it's crusted with
razor-sharp barnacles. *Ouch!*
                                        Great! You're in!
What do you see? *Everything's dark.*   Not quite.
A little light,   maybe from the blowhole,
is glinting off row upon row   of wicked teeth.
But whales don't....   Never mind, son; this is art!
Your job is to make that fake   whale as real
as you want to be yourself.
                                        Imagine
how the scene will play: your spotlit face,
terrified but resolute,   up on the screen.
Your audience   is with you; the whole house
is openmouthed—   not a whisper, not a crunch.
They're there   because they want to believe.
If you can only
                    connect, they'll follow you
all the way down.   "Behold now behemoth,
which I made with thee. He eateth...."   *Me!*

Bingo! Now *live* it! Hold   your nose; make them smell
that foul, fishy breath.   They'll wince when you trip
over the hummocky taste buds,   shudder
as you lose your grip

                        on the uvula and lurch
down the gullet. Your clothes   are soggy and heavy
with saliva, but still   you soldier on
because your heart's desire   (*What's that?* Shhh.... You'll
   see.)
is guaranteed   —it's in the script!—to be
festering somewhere   in that celluloid
belly. *Like an ulcer?*   Like a pearl.

THE CONSCIENCE OFF DUTY

Sure, the cricket   made himself a name
with the virtue bit.   But once he'd punched the clock?
Let me tell you   about the night I just
happened to drop   into the Toddy Tree,
a seedy dive   way out the Boulevard
where the leaf-chewers roost.

                       It's dark, it's funky—
pollen on the floor,   a rowdy crowd
of yellow jackets   jostling at the bar.
Down front, a hot combo   of katydids
is getting on the jive—   "Ain't Misbehavin'"—
really kicking out,   with a wolf spider
beating the skins. I scan the mob

                       and do
a double take: Is it?   It can't be. Yes.
Alone at a table,   knocking back shots
of honeydew—the "conscience"!   Just my luck!
He's lost the topper,   and his collar's askew,

but there's no mistaking   that deacon's mug.
I duck

         back into the shadows as the sax
lets out a long   wolf whistle, and a spot
comes up center stage.   What's the attraction?
All I can see   is something like a mummy
till the tempo hots up,   and the plain brown wrap
gives a little shiver.   Whatever's
inside is starting to move.

                       A seam at the top
unzips   (the cricket's leaning forward,
ogling like mad),   and a slick little head
pokes out. Antennae   unfurl and flutter: It's
Vanessa ("Painted Lady")   Virginiensis,
queen of the hootchy-kootchy,   and she's about
to do a peel.

             She gives a sort of lazy
full-body shrug,   and—Mama!—get a load
of that mummy now!   One tiny foot slides
out of the silk,   then slowly a whole
delicate black gam,   and another, and
another. . . .   In the pit, the licorice sticks
are swinging wide,

                and ripple after ripple
of shimmery chrysalis   is slipping, real
leisurely, to the floor.   She turns her sleek
thorax full into the light,   so it gleams
like jet.   Look at that cricket, licking his
desiccated mouthparts!   This is the guy
with the eighteen-carat badge?

                    "When the urge
is strong,"   they tell me, "give a little whistle!"
For *him*?   I know, I know—it's just an act.
But sometimes he seems so   *human*, I forget.

How can he spend his days   preachifying,
then this?   Tomorrow morning, he'll be Mr.
Holier-Than-Thou again,
                              but now—
under the table   I can see him rubbing
his brittle little   exoskeletal
legs together   as Vanessa stretches
out all her long limbs   and finally unfolds
her sticky scarlet wings.   The nectar must
be getting to me,
                         because suddenly
my stomach—the stink   of God only knows
what insect secretions,   the click-click-click
of hundreds of mandibles   grinding weed....
My head is buzzing, I can't breathe.   I shove
my way out through the jitterbugs   and make it
home somehow.
                         I swear, there ought to be a law
against the moonshine at that joint.   All night
I'm sweating and thrashing,   trying to wake up
from this idiotic dream: I'm stuck
in the wrong picture.   Everyone insists
that I'm Snow White.   So I try, but the costume
itches like a son of a bitch,
                              and the dwarfs
keep groping me.   (There seem to be more
than seven, and they've got   too many legs.)
The Blue Fairy's there,   but she's different, too,
leering like a two-bit tart,   and instead
of a wand,   she has an apple in her hand.
I tell her no dice—
                         that's not in the script!
I want my agent!   But the cricket winks,

and next thing I know   I'm flat on my back,
paralyzed.   What's that reek, like cheap perfume?
Who's that Beast   crouched in a thicket? My bed
is overgrown with roses   and the wrong
pair of lips
                    is hovering above me.
If only I could keep   everything closed!
But it's too late;   the garden is infested.
Invisible thighs   are stridulating
under every leaf.   I feel feelers
flick across my cheek.   The lips pucker.
This is the end   of my hundred years' sleep.

PINOCCHIO ON LOCATION

The DP is apeshit: "I told you guys
we got to get   some light into this belly!"
Word just came down   that yesterday's dailies
went straight to the floor,   and naturally now
the whole production crew   is scrambling
to say, "I told you so."
                              So the gaffer goes
for more carbon arcs,   and the rest of us
settle back in.   That old dope Geppetto
is trying to reheat   coffee on his little
Sterno-can stove.   A couple of the hands
are playing gin,   but it's almost too dark
to read the cards.
                         It's dark enough to sleep,
but too uncomfortable—   like an endless
intercontinental   flight in Economy.
I wrap myself   tighter in a clammy

sound blanket,   and try to be lulled by the hum
of the generating unit   parked
in the duodenum.
                        Walt? He's off
in his trailer,   probably on the horn
with the money men,   negotiating for
more time in the whale.   Great. The Jonah jokes
are already old.   *How long, oh Lord?* Who knows.
He never shows   until the actual
shooting starts, if then.
                        This is, what? Day six?
Or maybe even seven?   What a waste!
For a fraction of the cost,   we could have rented
a nice sound stage.   But no—Mr. *Artiste*
insists   on the genuine article.
He says we'll all   be so inspired, we'll sweep
the Oscars.
                    You wish it, pal. Morale
is lousy. Plus we're stale.   Sitting here,
going over and over   my lines, I'm
gradually losing   any feeling
I might once have had for this part: "FA-ther!" [pause]
"At LAST!"   [reach out, trembling a little,
work up a few tears]
                        "I've FOUND you!" No good.
How about: "I've—I've—"   [quaver, extra-long
pause, then almost   whisper] *"found* you." Worse and
    worse.
Let's face it; the scene   is hopelessly cornball,
and I can't blame Hollywood;   the hokum
is genuine.   Remember (I forget
myself, after all these years)
                        it was *my*
story.   Did I really find my way

in here, and—more   important—out again?
Did I actually care   about the old man?
At least back then   I had some motivation.
I was so hot   to get real, I'd say anything
and mean it. Now?
               Now I've hit the big time,
and here I am, back in the gut,   reading lines
that—real or not—are just   screaming for
a script doctor, but you're not   going to catch
anyone from the Guild   schlepping down that throat
for a last-minute fix.   The best boy says this game
is all about waiting.
         So OK. I'll close
my eyes,   do my breathing exercises,
and visualize   opening night: my name
in six-foot flashing letters   on the marquee!
A red carpet   (not a fifty-yard tongue)
unrolls—velvet cordons on   golden poles
barely hold back
               slithering, silver-sequined
shoals—please! no fish!—flocks   of starlets! I step
out of the black   stretch limo. Smell the Chanel!
(Block out the reek   of half-digested plankton.)
Flashbulbs pop.   The crowd is going wild! Just listen
to that applause!   It's roaring towards me, swelling,
about to break like a—No!
            I'm awake,
and the flabby walls   are pulsing; the grips
are sloshing after drifting props.   Goddamn it,
I thought we had a clause   explicitly
nixing peristalsis!   Where are our lawyers?
Back on dry land, of course.   The clapboard bobs by,
opening and shutting,
           but the viscous tide

isn't about to stop   rising. How did I
get us out of this before?   I used smoke
to make the monster sneeze.   But who'd believe
that nowadays?   Anyway, Geppetto's
little fire's washed out,   and the gastric juices
are already eddying   around my knees.

THE CRICKET CONVERTS

They brought in the conscience   as comic relief:
a pumpkin-headed   lowlife off the street
who'd drifted into   the rectitude racket
for the dough   and because he had the hots
for the Blue Fairy.   And did the cricket
ever fit the part!
                    A fat lot he knew
about the strait and narrow!   When he refused
a stunt double and hopped   right in through
the toy-shop window   first take, no sweat,
it was obvious   he'd put in a stint
as a second-story man.   And when he picked
the lock on the birdcage?
                    That was for real!
But in this biz we get all kinds.   In fact,
a little   extracurricular
education can even   give a guy
an edge,   so we're broad-minded. We figure,
as long as he's still got his chops   and shows up
sober, who cares?
                    But then a few weeks
into shooting, he changed.   His stogie was gone.
He started drinking coffee   on the coffee breaks,
and delivering   Methodist spiels

about his "character"   and "motivation."
We thought he must have met   some pointy-heads
over at the Brown Derby.
                              You know the type:
they're on the john,   the house is burning down,
and they're still doing   the gestures, the voice.
Fucking insufferable.   You'd ask him—
perfectly innocent—   what time it was,
and he'd start in   on how it was never
too late to repent.
                          Of course for me this meant
nonstop nag, nag, nag.   Say I had a rough night
and didn't make it   to the studio
quite on the dot—   if I mentioned that traffic
was bad (it was!),   I'd get a poke
in the ankle from his umbrella,   and he'd point
meaningfully at my nose.
                              Was it a joke?
That's what was creepy!   None of us could tell
if this gospel-gab   was on the level
or pure Stanislavski, or   some sicko gag.
But he'd suck you in!   I mean, technically
no one could touch me now;   I'd been real
for years, free and clear,
                              but man, did he know
what buttons to push!   If I muffed a cue,
he'd be tapping his head,   mouthing: "Wood!"
And during the bonfire scene,   he grabbed
a flaming stick,   chirping, "Woe unto Tinseltown!
Consider this flimsy   timber, how it burns,
like the eternal fire…"
                              and so on, even though
we all were giving him   the old razoo.
It didn't faze him;   he'd jump somewhere where we

couldn't swat him, and go on.   "Because you would not
   hear,
the sword, the famine,   and the pestilence
shall be visited upon you.   You shall be
a curse and an astonishment
                              and an hissing
and a reproach   among all the nations!"
An hissing? Where the hell   did he get this stuff?
And talk about "a pestilence"!   That insect
was a one-man plague!   It finally got so bad,
whenever he came on the set,   someone would yell,
"Quick Henry, the flit!"
                              But the worst was when
he'd catch me alone.   He must have gotten hold
of Collodi   because he had the dope
on some of the less   heartwarming episodes
that Disney cut.   "How's your investment?"
he'd ask, deadpan,   "That Field of Miracles
paying off yet?"
                    Ha ha. So I admit
I was young, I was dumb.   I bought the fox's pitch
about burying   my five gold talents
and waking up   to an overnight orchard
dripping doubloons.   Does he have to rub it in?
Or else he'd fix those big   bug eyes on me
all sorrowful-like, and sigh,
                              "Your poor old dad!
Remember how he sold   his coat to buy you food
and then you had him slapped   into stir on a phony
child abuse rap?   Poor man—he never quite
got over that, did he?"   Then he'd hop away,
and I couldn't focus   on my lines the whole
rest of the day.
                    Even after all these years,

I still can hear   some of his nasty cracks
when I'm lying half-awake   at 3 a.m.
It's like I'm back onstage   and the house is packed,
but I'm made of wood again   and my lips won't move.
I can see the hotshot   reviewers snickering,
and then they all walk out   before intermission.

PINOCCHIO ON WISHES

"When you wish upon a star...."   Oh, god,
that schmaltzy song!   I'll tell you something: if
I could do it all   over again, I'd wish
that that busybody   Blue Fairy had kept
her nose out of my business.   When I said
I wanted to be real,

                              what did I know?
I was only a punk kid,   a hunk of wood
slated to be a table leg.   Of course
I thought I was too good   for furniture,
so I bought into the hype,   took tap and voice,
and worked my butt off   until I made it
to marionette.

                         But being a hit
on the puppet circuit   wasn't enough.
Maybe you had to be there   to understand
the atmosphere: the promises, the pressure:
"No request   is too extreme!" the line went.
Now I'd say,   "Why the hell not? If everyone got
their heart's desire,

                              the world would be a mess!"
But back then, real was the thing.   I saw myself
in Technicolor flesh-and-blood,   playing
Gary Cooper–type roles.   I auditioned,

I nagged my agent, waited by the phone—   finally
the Fairy waved her wand   and I became
a real boy.

　　　　　Only no one ever told me
what real was going to mean.   Back at the toy shop,
I never had to fret   about the future;
when I fell asleep   in front of the fire
and burned off my feet,   all I had to do
was holler,   and the old man fixed me up
good as new.

　　　　　Even when I hit the road,
nothing could touch me.   I got sprung from jail
on a technicality,   sweet-talked my way
out of a stew pot.   When muggers left me hanging
from an oak tree,   the Fairy came through
and cut the rope.   My narrowest escape
was when Lampwick and I

　　　　　　　　overdid it a bit
on Pleasure Island and turned   into donkeys.
A greedy ringmaster   made me jump through hoops
until I went lame,   then tied me to a millstone
and dumped me in the sea.   Lo and behold!
A shoal of fish   nibbled off my donkey flesh,
and set my puppet skeleton

　　　　　　　　free again.
Lampwick wasn't so lucky.   When I saw him
years later, in a stable,   I had no clue
that the bag of bones   slumped in the stinking straw
was him, until I heard my name   whispered
in donkey lingo.   Yes, I saw the welts
the whip had raised.

　　　　　And yes, I saw the flies
dipping their tongues   into the moist sores
the harness   had eaten into his back.

I heard him breathing fast, gasping—   but what
could I have done?   Ever since my dream came true,
the Fairy has refused   to take my calls.
We're all on our own.

                        Like I told that Lost Boy
who cadges change   outside the Spinning Teacups,
trying to raise his fare   back to Neverland:
"You wished yourself out   of your fairy tale, friend.
Whose fault is it   if you forgot to read
the fine print? *No returns.*   Wishing won't get you
anywhere anymore.

                        The stars are for
decorative purposes only.   Ever after
ain't what it used to be—   no pot of gold,
no princess, no throne.   Just the moral: *caveat
emptor.*   Your heart's desire is guaranteed
to bite you in the ass,   and if you're happy,
brother, you can bet   it's not the end."

High Enlightenment

(based on Robert Darnton's Mesmerism and the End
of the Enlightenment in France*)*

By 1784, when it was demonstrated
"that water is not water but actually air,"
aeronauts had already soared
above the steeples, and Robespierre
had taken his first public stand
in defense of lightning rods.

                     On a sunny afternoon
in the Bois de Boulogne, chains of ladies
swayed along a long conductive silken cord
looped loosely around their
equators, linking them via harmonic fluids
to mesmerized trees.

                     Scientists watched bluebells
breathing in their sleep, and observed
the uncountable herds
of little donkeys kicking up
their heels in a single drop
of donkey semen.

                     Mirabeau revealed
that Frederick II had fathered
a centaur by consorting with a mare.
Up and down the boulevards, in all the cafés,
citizens were eating balloon *dragées*,
reading *Nouvelles*

                du monde lunaire
and a special illustrated
report from Prosper Voston on the first
documented harpy, shown
strangling a bull with one
of its flexible tails.

They mobbed the chessboard,
peered on tiptoe, whispered, shook
their heads as the wooden hand
of de Kempelen's robot jerked a rook
to check and mate.
The dancing egg jumped out
                              of the hat on command
and "a new principle, based on ricochets"
would soon enable a man in elastic shoes
to walk across the Seine. Styptic water
for haemorrhage; a paste of bread
and opium for gout.
                         Intellectuals
had given up snuff, which impairs
the delicate magnetic balance
of the nose. In mirror-lined,
velvet-curtained rooms, the watery tones
of a glass harmonica poured
                              over vitalized tubs
where doctors in lilac taffeta robes palpated
Lafayette's poles with silver wands, until
his hypochondria quivered
and he writhed on the carpet in
curative convulsions.
                         Celebrate
the new alliance of galvanic forces:
matter, movement, God.
A boy with a limp was thrown
into a pool with an electric eel
and emerged healed.
                         Soon mankind
would leave heavy, malevolent influences behind.
See the Little Master Physicist inflate
his breeches and cuffs; the crown

of his wide-brimmed hat is another
harlequin balloon.
                        All his mistresses
and creditors are clamoring below
and farther below. He waves his umbrella and taps
a few silent steps
on a cloud with his tapered toes.
Rise with him—but beware!
                        Sometimes the phlogisti-
    cated
air will catch. The crimson silk
and wicker gondola will kindle and fall
to earth as burning rain.
Even the great Pilâtre, France's hero,
went down in flames.
                        The Channel
was too wide after all,
the winds too strong.
"Il fut sourd à ma voix, et, comme un autre Cassandre,"
lamented Marat, *"je criai*
dans le désert."
                        Study the properties
of inflammable ethers before you leave the ground.
A child's kite and an ordinary key
will bind you in an animated circuit
to the beating heart of the sky. Purple clouds resound:
Aspire! Ascend
                        into the infiniverse! Test
the electric machines of your lungs
with ever purer, more
rarefied infusions of heretofore
unimagined air. Discover the laws
of passionate

              gravity. In the words
of Fourier's table, which spoke for him
after his death, thumping one foot
emphatically, "Yes, yes, yes. Aromatic
pipe. Conduit. Aromatic pipe. Conduit. Conduit.
Conduit. Conduit. Yes."

Frequently Asked Questions About Spirit Photography

Suggested by an exhibit at the Metropolitan Museum of Art in New York, and drawing on material from the accompanying catalogue, The Perfect Medium: Photography and the Occult *(Chéroux, Fischer, Apraxine, Canguilhem, and Schmit), as well as from* Ghosts in Photographs *(Fred Gettings),* Psychic Photography: Threshold of a New Science? *(Hans Holzer), and* Spook: Science Tackles the Afterlife *(Mary Roach)*

1. Is There a Scientific Explanation for What We Call "Ghosts"?

Not yet, but we are getting very close.   While some researchers
are studying the language of the gene,   learning how we become
the complicated physical creatures   we currently are,
others are investigating our   post-corporeal forms,
and may soon be able to answer   the age-old questions:
Where do specters come from?   What can we do to summon them
or to keep them away?

        Some old-fashioned "miasmists" still hold
that the familiar nebulous revenant   "merely represents
a record of past events   that somehow got left behind
in the atmosphere," a sort of lingering   optical echo.
Most current scholarship, however,   supports the persistence
of what we might informally call   "consciousness," and thus
"the survival   of a human personality
in a thought world."

        Our understanding of the manifold
and protean nature of matter   has grown exponentially
in recent centuries.   The work of Röntgen and the Curies
spurred the effluvists to experiment   with sensitized plates
which could pick up the "psychic,"   "neuric," "critical," "ceramic,"
"N-," "V-," or "Y-rays" that emanate   from the living brain,

and modern imaging techniques   will soon enable us
to trace the activity of these vital rays

                                        even after
metabolic function has ceased.   We may be almost
ready to test   what Gary Schwartz, founder of the Human
Energy Systems Laboratory   at the University
of Arizona, refers to as   "the death hypothesis."
The laws of thermodynamics   tell us that energy
is never lost;   rather, it passes into some other
component of the system.

                              "Death," then, is the conversion
of the vital force into some new   but still detectable state.
Hans Holzer, head   of the Center for Paranormal Studies, Inc.,
asserts that "man's personality,   or soul, if you prefer,
is also, in its strictest sense,   an electromagnetic
energy field, and as such   is capable of registering
on certain instruments,   some already in existence,
some as yet to be built."

                              Barometers, hygrometers,
photographic film, magnetographs,   Geiger counters, and countless
other devices have already   yielded promising results.
Following a long tradition   of measuring the weight
lost by the body when the soul departs,   Matla and van Zelst
captured "man-force" in a test tube   and computed its volume
at 36.7   cubic milliliters, based
on how much grain alcohol it displaced.

                              Meanwhile, field workers
continue to pursue   their invaluable observations
of phantoms *in situ*,   drawing on the ancient wisdom
of exorcists, "ghost-busters"   and others whose business it is
to rid human habitations   of disruptive spirits.
Though couched in the crude   idiom of superstition,
these folk beliefs include   valid insights into the nature
of psychic energy.

                    Empirical evidence long ago
established that spectral   manifestations are most
frequent in "areas of emotional   turmoil," and that moist
air conducts more readily than dry,   which accounts for why
"hauntings" often occur   in dank churches and houses deserted
in the wake of some unspeakable event.   It also explains
why ghosts do not seem to appear   at random, but in response
to some conscious or unconscious human overture.

                                                        Holzer notes
that "religious fervor, prayer,   incantations and strong desire
are all forms of thought projection—   the actual sending out
of small particles of energy,   each particle charged,
as it were, with a mission."   In an old stone cathedral,
thick walls, weak ventilation   and filtered light create ideal
conditions for a field   to persevere in a stable,
low-energy state until

                    the spiritual exertions
of supplicants boost it into   the visible spectrum;
high in the nave, a gaseous mass,   indistinguishable
at first from the incense,   takes on the visage of someone
someone holds dear,   growing more substantial with every orison.
When the service ends,   and worshippers' thoughts slacken and return
to everyday concerns,   it slowly dissipates, still pulsing
to the recessional.

                    By the same token, overwhelming fear
can bring into being the very   threat from which we flee.
The agitation of a lone   pedestrian forced to pass
a graveyard at night activates   dormant malevolent powers.
When we fully grasp this process   we will no longer need
to whistle in the dark;   we will have the capacity
to neutralize negative vibrations   and purge the earth
of unwelcome specters.

                    As for those discarnate entities
which we wish to keep with us,   they will now be forever

at our disposal.   Special transmitters and receivers
will eliminate the need for litanies,   séances, spells,
and other inefficient   and unreliable
methods of invocation.   In the foreseeable future
everyone will have the means   to make a given spirit
materialize as easily as we   now turn on a TV.

2. Isn't It Wrong to Summon Ghosts?

                                        Many see sciomancy
("the raising of the shades of the dead")   as blasphemous or worse.
We defy divine decree   if we attempt to extend
a soul's time on earth beyond the span   ordained by the Almighty.
Shame, they say,   on those who use dark arts to cajole or coerce
a departed spirit from   the fragrant fields of Elysium
back to our world of toil and tears and clay.   This is sorcery,
Satan's work.
                        Some accept séances but frown upon
taking pictures of the specters,   asserting that this practice
"has macabre and unhealthy undertones"   because it blurs
"the distinction between the natures   of this world and the next."
Visual images recall   the discarded physical shell,
but the soul is ethereal.   Ghost photography is thus
"shrouded in a subtle   materialism," distasteful
to true spiritualists.
                        There are dangers as well.
Burgeoning interest in communication   with astral beings
has led to a profusion of mediums,   some of whom
are ill-prepared to cope   with the discarnate powers they invoke.
In order to reach the planes   where supernal souls dwell,
a medium must learn   to accelerate her own vibrations.
Until then, her commerce   will be limited to heavier presences,
"unprogressed spirits," which may have agendas

at odds with ours.
Fred Gettings warns, "it must be clearly grasped that not all the forces
of the invisible world   are working for the spiritual
evolution of man."   The nether levels of the aether
teem with *diakka* and other   low-grade agencies,
which are notoriously   eager to converse.
They "will promise much   but are capable of granting nothing
of real human value."

Our impatience for a glimpse
beyond the grave leads us   to forget what serious occultists
have always emphasized: "a manifesting 'spirit'
may be exactly what he professes to be,   but on the whole
the probabilities are that it   is nothing of the kind."
The grieving parents   who weep with joy at the apparition
of their smiling child   are all too frequently the victims
of a demonic hoax.

After a successful séance or two,
the *diakka* may weary of their game,   and the false image
will simply cease to materialize,   leaving loved ones
frantic with thwarted hope.   Crueler still, the hitherto benign
visitations may change in tone.   Widowers have been driven
to suicide when the seeming shades   of their faithful wives
have taunted them   with lubriciously elaborated fictions
of infidelity.

The spirits lead us down a slippery slope
from credulousness to foolish elation,   then doubt,
which quickly turns to bitterness, despair,   and loss of faith.
Furthermore, once we open the door   to the incorporeal,
we have no control   over who uses it. While we sit
gawking at a specter, who knows   what uninvited entities
may be taking advantage   of this temporary portal
to steal, unnoticed, back to earth?

And is it in the best interests
of the spirits themselves   to reestablish contact

with earthbound persons?   Hans Holzer believes that the most
easily invoked are those   who are "unable to adjust"
to their new state of being   in "the world of the mind."
The ghosts we see are artifacts   of their struggle to remain
in their bodies, "unaware   that they no longer exist
on the physical plane."

                              One medium describes such "stuck souls"
as "roaming around   looking for someone alive to be with,
attracted by warmth."   Some say we are doing them a kindness
when we enable them, however briefly,   to be heard and seen.
"A human personality   'hung up' in time and outside space"
suffers its own bereavement,   so a séance brings solace
not only to those who have been left behind   but also to the
imperfectly passed away.

                              Others oppose what they call
an unhealthy   "interdimensional codependency."
The duty of the living is to live   in the here and now.
The duty of the dead is to move on.   We must not cling
to their fading shadows   or encourage them to linger
on the outskirts of this world,   when they should be ascending
through spheres of ever-purer   insubstantiality
into astral light.

                              But if the Lord himself has left this loophole
in the veil that divides   mortal from immortal, isn't He
implicitly permitting   discourse between the realms?
Or is the very possibility   of transgression a test
like the apple?   Indications are ambiguous.
So if you are unsure   whether or not to attempt to reach
someone beyond, we can only say,   "Look searchingly
into your own heart.

                              What are your motives, and how much
are you willing to risk?"   If your desire to see the departed
is untainted by base impulses,   and if your resolve is firm,
you may be able to withstand   the rapture of a dark half hour

with (perhaps) your beloved,   knowing full well that the words
whispered by those pale lips   may be lies, and that if,
unhinged by the vision, you try   to stroke the hair, your heavy hand
will slice through the gossamer   skull like an ax, feeling nothing.

3. What Is "Ectoplasm"?

This blanket term, literally meaning
"outward form," covers a range   of immaterialities
temporarily rendered visible   by the medium.
Classically, it manifests   as "a white viscous substance
with an ozone-like smell"   emanating from her mouth, nose,
or other orifices.   The popular appellations
for the most common classes   include *cheesecloth*, *spittle*,
cobweb, and *bridal veil.*
The shapes ectoplasm assumes
are almost as diverse as those   of terrestrial life.
It is now widely believed   that the many varieties,
although they may share basic building blocks,   are no more like
one another than an amoeba   is like you or me.
But our knowledge is still   frustratingly limited
because of the great difficulty   of obtaining samples
for analysis.
One well-established characteristic
of ectoplasm is that it disappears   the instant it
is exposed to most types of light.   Collection attempts
have also been hindered by the fact   that the material
usually remains "closely attached   to the medium, both
physically and psychically."   When the great pioneer
of spirit research, Albert von Schrenck-Notzing,   tried to grasp
a "fine rubber string"

emerging from the medium known
as "Eva C.," she "gave a cry of pain.   He then forbade
himself any violent extraction,"   which would clearly pose
"a danger to the medium's health."   Those few specimens
that have been retained   and examined with a polariscope
have been shown to consist of "albuminoid   and fatty matter"
which can almost always be   genetically identified
with the medium.
                        The implications of these findings
are hotly debated,   and the issue is complicated
by the fact that ectoplasm   can evolve over the course
of a séance. The first sign   may be a concentrated gleam,
a kernel   of light from which luminous tendrils then
extend into the darkened room.   Sometimes a patch of haze
gathers above the medium's head   and hardens into whiteness,
like the moon as the day fades.
                            Usually the process ends there;
but if the psychic rays   are strong enough, these primitive
manifestations grow more complex.   The most famous cases
are those in which the homogeneous   nimbus develops
into the semblance of a face   with the identifiable
features of a person   who has departed this world.
These are the "ghosts" whose images   are sometimes captured
by spirit photographers.
                        On other occasions
the diaphanous mass   solidifies to such an extent
that it can be "utilized   via thought direction
to perform some intelligent task."   Channeling the energy
generated by her family's   fervent performance
of spiritualist hymns,   Kathleen Goligher was able
to move heavy tables   by means of powerful "psychic rods"
extruded from between her legs.

Plasmic emanations
require both intense   emotional stimulation
and strenuous physical effort   on the medium's part.
She often undergoes   great suffering, and writhes about in throes
reminiscent of childbirth,   or performs bizarre actions
at the urging of her "spirit guides."   One thorny problem
for scholars is the role   of these discarnate beings in
ectoplasmogenesis.
                         Some say the medium merely
provides the raw material   which the spirits harvest
for their own purposes,   but most assign her greater agency.
Schrenck-Notzing argued   "that mediumistic activity
was akin   to the process of artistic creation
and that the formation   of materializations
proceeded from a real   'Kunstwollen,'" a primal drive
to make a work of art.
                         He observed that "some ideoplasties
are rough dilettante sketches,"   while others are clearly the fruit
of a "supreme   artistic intelligence." Early
in her career, Eva C.   produced only the crudest
ectoplasmic forms: sticky strings   hanging from her erect nipples,
or a damp, cold pseudopod   which sprouted from her navel,
then rose into the air and swayed   "in broad undulations
like a living reptile."
                         Her later style was far more refined.
Photographs obtained   by placing cameras inside
the spirit cabinet   reveal the life-sized, loosely veiled
face of a beautiful woman   "of the oriental type"
superimposed on her own.   Schrenck-Notzing comments
that the visage "has something animal, cruel,   wild about it;
the half-open mouth,   the seemingly painted lips suggest
a strong sensuality."
                         Was Eva C. mere putty
molded by disembodied hands,   or did her own spirit

help shape these haunting portraits?   Many see in them evidence
of what Flournoy   called the "subliminal imagination,"
later better known as Freud's "unconscious."   They say she harnessed
some transcendent force,   the "od" or "penetrating all," to knead
her own clay   into images of her ordinarily
inaccessible ideas

                        —or perhaps those of her audience.
All the ambient   psychic activity in the room
may help shape the protean plasmic matter.   Like a battery,
the medium picks up this charge,   converting it into current,
and the resulting field is visible   to the human eye.
This would explain   why many apparitions represent
persons unknown to the medium herself,   but intimately
linked with someone else at the séance.

                                    Many others, however,
seem to communicate with   the medium alone.
The famous "Margery,"   wife of a distinguished surgeon,
would speak in the "hoarse, masculine   disembodied voice"
of her "controlling spirit,"   an entity identified
as her elder brother Walter, who had died   in an accident.
His ectoplasmic form   consisted of a long thin wrist
and a small rubbery hand.

                        Walter permitted flash photography,
so we have an extensive record   of his appearances;
sometimes he emerged   from one of Margery's nostrils or ears,
sometimes from between her thighs.   One striking stereoscopic view
shows her naked from the waist down,   except for a small towel
for modesty, her legs spread wide,   and her hands securely held
away from her body by assistants   to prevent deception.
Walter's ectoplasmic arm

                        is issuing from her navel;
his hand seems to be very soft,   with short, pudgy fingers,
and resembles a starfish   crawling across the white
towel towards her loins.   We also have a picture of the thumbprint

which he left (at his own suggestion)   in a basin
of heated dental wax.   It was later found to match
a print on the handle   of a razor, among his belongings
in his mother's attic.

                            Was this, as Walter himself
and others claimed, the long-sought   "proof of human immortality"?
Was the hand (which Margery always   reabsorbed before the end
of the séance) part of Walter or of her?   Was Schrenck-Notzing right
when he stated, "To touch this substance   is to touch her life"?
As more specimens   are studied with advanced instruments,
we will come closer   to grasping the origin and nature
of these "psychicons,   luminous living images of thought."

4. WHY DO SOME MEDIUMS HIDE IN BOXES?

                                    The word "hide" reflects
a common prejudice: many distrust the darkness
necessary for a séance,   and suspect that the "box"
(more properly *spirit cabinet*)   conceals apparatus
with which the medium produces   fraudulent effects.
But the sad fact that trickery   does, on occasion, take place
should not be exploited by skeptics   to cast doubt on the vast
majority of honest mediums.

                            Do the sham nostrums
of a few quacks   invalidate the whole medical profession?
Of course not. We offer our arms   to the vaccinator's needle,
grateful that a specialist   is somehow able to save us
from invisible attackers.   We do not dismiss
the chemist's laboratory   as a hall of smoke and mirrors.
As for darkness, we acknowledge   that an astronomer
must make his observations at night.

                            Spirit phenomena,
like distant stars,   are best discerned against the blackest backdrop.

And, unlike stars, they are   exquisitely photosensitive,
dissipating instantly   at the cameraman's flash.
In fact, the photographer's art   provides a fair analogy
to that of the medium;   the production of an image
requires, at every stage,   conditions close to those in which
spirits materialize.

Henry Irving asks, "What would we reply
to him who would say: I believe photography   is a humbug,
do it all in the light,   and we will believe otherwise?"
Some scholars suggest   that the medium actually serves
as a sort of "developer":   upon contact with her,
the activated spectral matter   is made manifest
to the human eye,   though only briefly, as we have not yet
found a fixative.

Others compare the spirit cabinet
to a *camera obscura*,   and the medium's mind
to a light-admitting lens.   The transcendental rays enter, then
are bent and focused;   if this refracted beam is strong enough,
an image will take shape.   But the first and greatest problem
is to attract the astral forms   back to the earthly plane
which they have abandoned,   generally without regret,
for the "summerland."

Most immaterial beings
are revolted by the sight, sound, and smell   of terrestrial
bodies like those to which they were once chained—   lumps of flesh
that thump and thrash about within   three awkward dimensions.
They will thus respond to a summons   from this side only when
darkness and silence prevail,   the body is still, and the soul's
vibrations travel unimpeded   between worlds. This is why
most of us see spirits only in our dreams.

To capture these
fleeting apparitions   in photographs, we must create
a simulacrum of a sleeping creature   in the séance room.
The cabinet is thus a trap,   and the medium bait.

Strapped into her special garment,   half camisole, half straitjacket,
her ankles bound to her chair,   her wrists trussed behind her back,
her mouth stopped with a knotted rag,   and her whole head encased
in a heavy back hood,
                    she presents a disturbing figure.
Cynical witnesses assume   that this is all for show.
They think of Houdini, arch-foe   of spiritualism,
who believed only in agile fingers,   fastidious planning,
and a gullible public. His own career   was based on expertly
orchestrated suspense: his audience's   titillating fear
that this time he might not break free   of the elaborate shackles
he himself had devised.
                    But the medium does not escape.
The impresario   will not authorize her release
until a ghost has come and gone,   or until the spectators
lose patience and disperse,   declaring the séance a failure.
Her receptive faculties,   deprived of external stimuli,
turn inward and (it is hypothesized)   transmit a signal
attractive to immortals.   If conditions are right,
some curious soul will
                    sidle up to the margin of our
material sphere   to investigate this strange liminal
creature, immobilized in her little cell.   A discarnate
hand reaches into the pinpoint   aperture which her
artificially concentrated   consciousness has conjured.
Does she flinch at its touch?   The audience cannot see.
They see a shimmer, then a form resolving   like the negative
of a shadow when the sun slips out
                    from behind a cloud.
The photographer tugs on his cord,   the shutter opens,
magnesium blazes, and the shade   hastily retreats.
An assistant unlocks the cabinet;   unbound, the medium
flops to the floor, sweating and spent,   gasping as the gag
is cut from her mouth.   The photographer rushes to his darkroom,

and waits. The medium's fee   will depend on whether or not
the hoodwinked specter has left   its imprint on his plate.

5. How Can We Be Sure the Images Aren't Faked?

If what you seek
is guaranteed, risk-free authenticity,   then maybe
spirit photography is not for you.   Even ardent
spiritualists admit   that of the thousands of pictures
purported to represent   departed souls, only a few
really show ghosts.   Scam artists will always be with us,
so those believers who most urgently   yearn for concrete proof
must also be the most exacting skeptics.
When the French press
reported the first spirit photographs,   Allan Kardec,
editor in chief of the *Revue spirite*,   warned his readers
to "refrain from giving credence   to all the tales of wonder
that the enemies   of Spiritualism like to spread."
The movement would only progress   by keeping a scrupulous
distance from naïve enthusiasts   and conducting rigorous
scientific tests.
Psychic researchers should try to secure
concrete artifacts, like the plaster casts   of the ectoplasmic
miniature hands and feet   made manifest by Franek Kluski
under strict supervision   at the Insitut Métaphysique
International. Witnesses agreed   that when the lights
in the windowless laboratory were dimmed,   "a strong odor
of ozone could be smelled," and small   luminous limbs
floated through the air.
Upon request, the limbs obligingly
plunged into a basin of warm paraffin,   then disappeared,
leaving molds like waxen gloves and socks   one millimeter thick.
The exquisitely detailed casts made from these   were subjected

to anthropometric analysis   by the Department
of Judicial Identity of the Paris police;   no match
was found between the fingerprints   and those of anyone
attending the experiment.

                              The criminologist
Cesare Lombroso studied   Eusapia Palladino,
"queen of mediums," renowned   for her "physical effects."
He identified forty-six classes,   including "lights and knocks,
the billowing of fabrics,"   "the movement of various objects
without visible physical   intervention of any kind,"
the imprints of faces and hands,   and "partial or complete
levitations."

                    Many eminent figures, including
the astronomer Camille Flammarion,   Henri Bergson,
and Pierre and Marie Curie,   observed her at work in a series
of séances.   "The organizers used an entirely new
technological arsenal,"   measuring everything
from temperature, barometric pressure,   and humidity
to the impact of sonic vibrations   and the slightest
variations in electric or magnetic fields.

                                        They aimed
"to establish   what could be explained rationally,
and what remained irrational."   But because "the use of flash
made her ill,"   Palladino permitted photography
only rarely, and then only when   she herself "gave the signal
with a cry of 'Fuoco!'"   Thus, despite the "efforts of the most
illustrious scientists,   incontestable results
could not be obtained."

                        Albert von Schrenck-Notzing had more success
with the medium Eva C.,   who often worked naked,
"removing any possibility   of hiding [fake
materializations] in her clothing."   Female monitors
searched her body cavities,   and a stomatologist
eliminated the suspicion   of volitional

regurgitation by feeding her   "a black currant mixture
to tint her stomach red."

                              The emanations from her mouth,
as recorded from various angles   by nine single-lens
and stereoscopic cameras,   were all pure white, and often
the nebulosity   enfolded an identifiable
face from the dead.   Most researchers accepted this evidence
of an astral presence.   Detractors, however, detected
"a little opening"   in the cover of Eva C.'s chair,
where she "could have hidden pre-prepared pages."

                                        Perhaps she did.
But while there is no excuse   for fraud, those who actually produce
the false images   should not be made to shoulder all the blame.
Their patrons must ask themselves   what role their own insatiable
desire to see beyond the grave   has played in undermining
the medium's integrity   by treating the rare and precious
gift of a spirit's visit   like a commodity that should be
available at any time for purchase.

                              Spectral "extras"
are notoriously temperamental,   refusing to pose
on demand, so the medium knows   that, try as she may,
she will often disappoint her audience.   Eager always
to please, she may take out "insurance"   against those occasions
on which the ghosts do not cooperate.   If her subterfuge
is discovered, her followers   turn on her with the fury
of a lover betrayed.

                        Now they cynically dismiss
all spiritist claims   as fraudulent, but surely this
is as illogical   as unquestioning acceptance.
As Kardec says, "Fake diamonds take   nothing from the value
of real diamonds.   Artificial flowers do not prevent
there being natural flowers."   The very skepticism
that saves us from overcredulity   may cause us to fall
into the opposite error.

                      After exposing ninety-nine
acts of charlatanry, we may become   so callous, so afraid
of deception, that we fail   to recognize a genuine
message from beyond the veil.   But "dupery for dupery,"
asks William James,   "what proof is there that dupery from hope
is so much worse than dupery from fear?"   If our gleaming
positivist armor   is completely impermeable,
we will suffocate.

                      Consider the case of Édouard Buguet.
A professional photographer,   he was puzzled
when his portraits started   to be spoiled, sporadically,
by gauzy visages—   the result, he assumed, of improper
cleaning of the plates.   But when he showed these curious accidents
to his sitters, they reacted   with terror and joy,
recognizing the faces   "as those of dear departed."
Soon Buguet was famous

                      as a "*médium malgré lui*,"
and he found himself besieged   by legions of the bereaved
beseeching him for the solace   of a posthumous portrait.
They offered unheard-of fees; *le tout Paris*   clamored for ghosts.
Buguet learned to woo   the capricious spirits with music,
incantations, and "magnetic passes,"   but their responses
were still frustratingly   unreliable. In despair,
he turned to artifice.

                      When the police (who suspected a link
between spiritists and socialists)   raided his studio,
they discovered dummies, doll heads,   muslin veils, and more than
two hundred paper faces, varied enough   to supply nearly
any common type.   The state and the Church prosecuted the case
with a vengeance, though some clients   remained loyal, even after
his guilty plea, viewing the trial   as "a new Inquisition
or Galileo affair."

                      To escape his sentence, Buguet fled
to Belgium, where   he publicly "recanted his confession,"

but by now his career   had been irreparably damaged.
He went bankrupt, vanished,   then resurfaced years later, working
under a pseudonym;   his death went unrecorded.
Many scholars still hold   his early achievements in high esteem,
and lament the loss   of "a true spiritist gone bad
for lust of gold."

                    But the tragedy was less that he succumbed
to material temptation   than that (his recantation
notwithstanding) he seems   to have lost faith in his power
to summon the immaterial.   After his disgrace,
there were no more séances.   Never again would he wait,
breathless, wondering   whether or not the darkness would give way
to a stream of milky rays   that would quicken and converge
into form at his word.

                    Never again would he feel the thrum
of celestial vibrations   when he released the shutter.
The man who had served   as the "passive instrument" of forces
he did not pretend to understand now left   nothing to chance.
His later pictures are   impeccable phantasmagoria,
artfully composed and lit,   in perfect focus. No more
blurred half faces or   amorphous masses of astral matter
blotting out the sitter.

                    His clients no longer stare
blank-eyed into blackness, haggard with grief.   Now they recoil
in well rehearsed horror   from skeletons, ghosts, and devils
cavorting on a studio set.   To promote his new business,
he printed a series of "recreational   self-portraits," in which
he appears "in conversation   with his ethereal double . . .
and the specter of death."   In one image, entitled
Mysterious Communications,

                    Buguet, in evening dress,
sits sedately at a table,   immersed in a book,
ostentatiously oblivious   of the beautiful phantom
who hovers overhead,   displaying an advertisement

for his services: "Success assured. Invisible
manipulation carried out   in front of the client."
His new business card read: *Photographie antiSPIRITE.*
Le Spectre choisi est garanti.   ILLUSION COMPLÈTE.

6. What Is the Future of Spirit Research?

We are on the verge
of great breakthroughs. Consider how far   modern technology
has brought us already; we can observe   the birth and death
of distant stars,   and translate sound, heat, and magnetic force
into images,   so surely it is merely a matter
of time until we dismantle   once and for all the ancient
but artificial barrier   that separates the incarnate
from the discarnate realm.
The inextricable entanglement
of body and spirit   becomes clearer every day.
The thoughts of a rhesus monkey   can now lift the steel arm
of a robot halfway   around the world. Soon victims
of paralysis will tap   their brains' electrical impulses,
converting their ideas   via machine interface
into speech and action.   We may expect comparable progress
in our study of ghosts.
First, though, we must determine
the nature and origin   of spectral manifestations.
Are phantoms,   as "exogenists" assert, autonomous
entities temporarily   rendered perceptible?
Or, as "endogenists" argue,   are they simply our own
memories, dreams, and fears   externalized and projected
onto the visible spectrum   by means of mechanisms
as yet unknown?
This latter possibility is thrilling;
imagine the vast fund   of psychic energy locked up

in every cranium.   When we discover the key,
our whole world will change.   Just as today's schoolchild learns to master
the numbers and letters   with which we give visible form
to the products of our minds,   tomorrow's will be trained
to delineate persons and things   using the power
of thought alone.

                    And once we can project a visual likeness,
we will soon find a way to capture   other senses as well.
Today's wavery images will become   three-dimensional,
solid to the touch,   able to protect and comfort us.
Before we know it, we may be sharing   our physical space
with simulacra so real   that we will be hard put to tell
the difference between ourselves   and creatures composed of pure
will and imagination.

                    But if the exogenists are right,
and our so-called "ghosts" are real   beings of another order,
the implications for the human race   are even more profound.
New questions will arise: Are they always among us, unseen,
except under special conditions,   or do they dwell
on another plane   which now and then intersects with ours?
Are they, as all the evidence suggests,   the departed
spirits of the dead?

                    If so, do they linger forever
in an ethereal state,   or is this just one phase
in a (perhaps infinite) series   of transformations?
Establishing a channel   of discourse, of course, will be the first,
most urgent goal.   Scientists worldwide will vie to locate
a stable interplanar zone   where flesh and after-flesh
can meet on equal terms.   When we are able to communicate
with someone who has been dead 100 years,

                                        we will have crossed
what Hans Holzer calls "the greatest of all   remaining last frontiers."
Humanity's proudest   inventions and discoveries—the wheel,

electricity, flight, the splitting of the atom—   will pale
beside this new knowledge.   If every mind that has ever lived
is still accessible,   and each new generation can converse
with all their ancestors,   then no human accomplishment
is ever lost.

A woman wearing only a necklace of teeth
will show us the curative properties of a weed.   A busboy
will posthumously   publish his proof of Goldbach's conjecture.
A backwoods crackpot   whose children hauled his stacks of yellowed
    notebooks
to the dump unread,   will demonstrate how to harness a new
source of energy.   A slave whose tongue was cut out will tell her story.
With living and dead working together,   we will put an end
to poverty, discord, and disease.

Even more important,
the fear of death, which has oppressed   every human soul
since the dawn of consciousness,   will dissipate. Once we are sure
that the mind survives,   we will accept the loss of the body
with equanimity.   Departed spirits, finally back
in regular contact   with the mortal world, will be happier, too.
When they no longer feel   forgotten or misunderstood,
malicious hauntings will cease.

Although the currently incarnate
will probably not live to see this promise fulfilled,   we will still
reap its benefits from "the other side."   When we have a message
for our successors, we will not   need a medium.
We will not have to hurl   cushions and chairs around the room
to prove that we exist,   or dirty our astral fingers
laboriously scrawling luminous words   into the murky
terrestrial atmosphere.

Today's séances will stand
to tomorrow's transmortal dialogue   as the telegraph
(amazing in its day!) stands to the iPhone.   Just as we can
barely imagine   what life was like for our prehistoric

forebears, or how we could have been   ourselves in such a world,
our distant descendants, in their turn,   will wonder how we
could live as we do now.   The "bad old days," when living and dead
were separate, will seem remote beyond belief,

                                                       like tall tales
of atavistic terror   savored around a campfire
or bad dreams creeping up unbidden   from the unsupervised
recesses of our brains: terrors from our childhood or before—
the wrathful father; the troll under the bridge;   the sabertooth's cave;
the shades that wail   in eternal exile, hammering
against the veil;   the midnight chamber where a pale, restless shape
tosses, moans, and flails in its tangled sheet,   struggling to awake.

Feux d'artifice

*The poems in this sequence were suggested by an exhibit of
graphic representations of fireworks at the Metropolitan
Museum of Art, New York. They incorporate material from
the exhibition catalogue by Suzanne Boorsch (*Fireworks!*)
and from* Incendiary Art *by Kevin Salatino.*

ON ATTITUDES TOWARDS ALLEGORY

For centuries, no fireworks   display could take place
without allegory. Burke's   "splendid confusion"
was in fact quite schematic,   and the lexicon
of classical   devices still accessible
to the general public;
                              even the rabble
recognized the fire-breathing   lion of Lyon,
and understood   Apollo as a figure for
Louis XIV,   dolphins for the dauphin, a rock
for the Princess of Saxony.
                                   The actual
pyrotechnics   merely provided the climax
to a splendid and   didactic demonstration
of the glory and the power   of whatever
crowned head could currently claim
                                        divine endorsement.
The very stars would seem to burst   free of their spheres
to enlist in the service   of empire: serpents,
suns, and rains would rout   Cerberus, the Turks, the Dutch,
Huguenots, heretics, the Hun,
                                   even the Beast
of Revelation.   One role of the festival
was to mediate boundaries   "between, among
other things, the real   and the fictive . . . citizens
and regent."

According to Cahuzac, the best
model for a fireworks fête   was *Paradise Lost*.
"The attack, the battle, the fall . . .   the good angels'
moment of triumph"   were edifying as well
as entertaining.
                            "All spectacles represent
something. . . . The movement   of the most brilliant rocket
if it does not have a fixed   aim, displays nothing
but a trail of fire that vanishes   into thin
air."
            The same principle naturally applied
to commemorative prints,   which strove to convey
a scene's transcendent   significance, favoring
the metaphorical rather   than the mundane
literal "truth."
                        An ordinary market square
is transfigured.   The vegetable carts are gone.
Twelve vices, each identified   in Latin, burn,
and Virtue, rampant,   reigns at the center, astride
a chariot that
                        does not appear to be made
of papier-mâché.   Overhead, pillars of flame
erupt in a strict colonnade   and intersect
to decorative effect   with Catherine wheels
which whirl in perfect clockwork circles,
                                            their rims just
touching, creating   a fiery celestial frame
for the king's insignia.   At a shilling apiece,
such emblems   of imperial entitlement
sold prodigiously in their time.
                                But eternal
truths have fallen out of fashion,   and allusions
to the classical tradition   either are not
appreciated, or are   viewed with suspicion,

since they remind us
                              of what we now know to be
a heritage of rapacity.   We snicker
at Commerce, the Arts,   and Domestic Industry
clothed in togas,   bearing their little attributes
tucked in the crooks of their elbows, like toys.
                                                    Today's

sensibility rejects   the hieratic
and the excessively   symmetrical. We feel
that verisimilitude   entails exclusion
of received meanings,
                              and admire a measure of
dissonance. Images once   hailed by the critics
as paragons of composition   now rarely
rate a second glance.   A minutely detailed *Amor
Victor* with twin phoenixes
                                        exulting above
a Temple of Hymen is consigned   to long-term
storage, and Dumont's   engraving of the goddess
Isis atop a rainbow   spanning the summits
of two eighty-foot
                              Pyrenees (or "volcanoes")
and a rising sun (the Roi-Soleil)   all floating
on a large barge in the Seine   is dismissed as "a
rather tepid visual record,   unlikely
to impress."
                        Instead, we prize expressionistic
depictions, like Claude Lorrain's   view of the newly
elected King   of the Romans emerging from
a burning tower amidst   a black staccato
salvo of dashes and dots.
                                    The rockets' urgent
if indecipherable tracks   all but blot out
the Double-Headed Eagle,   the Crown, and the Four

Continents, which will not be   recognized, except
by a few cognoscenti.
                        But is even this
illegibility innocent   of meaning?
The gestural refusal   to recognize one
climactic moment   of universal order
is surely allegorical, too,
                        only more
constricted and self-absorbed   than the grand tableaux
of off-the-rack   equestrian saviors, high-waisted
lyre-strumming graces,   and hydra-headed tyrants
which we currently disdain.
                        Since authorities
are suspect, and no   perspective is now "correct,"
we have become our own sole   point of reference.
Historic events,   terror and jubilation,
combustion, motion, darkness and light
                                    are reduced
to vehicles   for the artist's incessantly
searching eye and hand.   A gusher of sparks pushes
into the sky but is stopped short   by the upper
edge of the page.
                        It splashes flat and ricochets
back down, dissolving,   while the insatiable crowd
waits for the next explosion.   This metaphor may
amuse us,   but we weary rapidly of such
a one-note trope.
                        Indeed, there are already signs
that our recent taste   for solipsism has passed
its peak.   The clotted, Pollock-like splatter we praised
yesterday is no longer   a revelation;
chaos and uncertainty
                        have become clichés.
Scholars call   our estrangement from traditional

values and our   omphaloskepsis typical
features of fin de siècle   anxiety
and ennui, and say we are due
                                            for something new.
What will it be?   We can imagine just so far:
a crowd on a beach;   a city in the background;
strange clothes, strange architecture,   but the faces raised
to the sky are familiar.
                              Above them, a huge
mythological creature   is incarnate for
a moment, in fire.   The watchers know what it means,
and smile in agreement. It seems   to be speaking
comfortable words
                                    directly to each of them.
This allegory   of the future is captured
in a future medium   and a future style
unknown to us, marvelous   in its minuteness
and vigor.
                        How will they do it? What disciplined
burin or brush or   virtual equivalent
will stroke their cheeks   with a breath from off an ocean
that does not exist?   And what intimate, distant
voice will still echo   in the bones of their story?

ON THE ACCURACY OF THE HISTORICAL RECORD

When we consider   all the commemorative
etchings, engravings,   and aquatints issued in
conjunction with state-sponsored   fireworks, we may ask
to what extent   these publications represent
what actually happened.
                                    Naturally, since
the exigencies of print   technology meant

that the historical record   must be composed
in advance of the event,   inaccuracies
often ensued,

                    but only occasionally
does a dissenting voice come down to us;   a note
in a margin, a few lines   in a journal or
letter attest   to discrepancies between plan
and execution.

                    Despite all the artistry
of the pyrotechnician,   when the medium
incorporates gunpowder,   a happy outcome
is far from assured.   Faulty fuses, rain, or high
humidity might

                    hinder ignition, and one
dropped match or unforeseen shift   in the wind would lead
to unscheduled combustion.   Although authorized
accounts elide   blunders such as this, some survive
in private reports.

                    The prodigious display staged
at Versailles to hail   the union of the future
Louis XVI and Marie Antoinette   was, we learn,
from several correspondents,   marred by violent
storms and choking smoke,

                         and two years later, in stark
contrast to sanctioned historians,   the blunt Duc
de Cröy described   the immensely expensive
fête saluting   the birth of their son, the dauphin,
as "a complete failure." Across

                    the Channel, too,
mishaps may well have   outnumbered unqualified
successes. While souvenir views   of the Royal
Fireworks that marked   the Treaty of Aix-la-Chapelle
depict the promised climax,

                    ("very beautiful

illuminations"), Walpole called them "pitiful
and ill-conducted, with no change of coloured fires
and shapes....Scarce anybody had patience to wait
for the finishing."
                    For those who remained, further
disappointments were in store. During the largo
of Handel's specially commissioned suite, a set
piece representing "Peace" malfunctioned, "and then what
contributed to
            the awkwardness of the whole
was the right pavilion catching fire and being
burned down in the middle of the show [though] very
little mischief was done and but two persons
killed."
        Even such serious hitches in the
festivities are most frequently forgotten,
erased by the mass-produced and extensively
disseminated official fictions, which tend
to outlive eyewitnesses.
                    Perhaps misplaced faith
in erroneous historical documents
led the current Crown Prince, Charles, and Diana, his
bride-to-be, to base their own wedding fireworks on
the very fiasco so
                scornfully dismissed
by Walpole over two hundred years earlier.
Or perhaps they hoped that a perfect performance
on the second try would cancel their ancestors'
embarrassment.
                Sadly, the location again
proved unlucky; the structure, this time intended
to burn, would not, and since news is now reported
live, the Royal Family was forced to rely
on the media's loyalty—

                          their readiness
to do their patriotic duty   and downplay
the incident discreetly.   With sufficient skill,
even an unsuppressable   mistake may be
turned to the state's advantage.

                          Take the great London
jubilee—complete   with simulated naval
battle on the Serpentine   and a revolving
castle that became   a temple—to celebrate
the Glorious Peace of 1814

                          (seven
months before Napoleon's   escape from Elba).
First a pagoda exploded.   Then a bridge burst
into inextinguishable   flames and collapsed.
However, since this accident

                          happened just when
the evening's entertainment   was reaching its peak,
the public assumed   that it was yet another
part of the program,   a notion not discouraged
by the sponsors.

                    This fortuitous solution
might not be feasible today.   But at that time,
the fashionable conception   of the sublime
entailed "obscurity, distant   danger and pain,
suddenness, loudness, and stenches."

                          A handbook on
"rational recreations"   supplied instructions
for constructing   (out of widely available
materials) a small but   active volcano
in the reader's own backyard;

                          the wilder the fire,
the more awful, and thus more   inspiring the art.
The fact that the conflagrations   in Saint James Park
were unexpected   in no way detracted from

their picturesqueness.

      They therefore were permitted
to enter the record, and even a modern
audience can appreciate the affecting
interplay of elements captured in Calvert's
popular print.

     Most of the scene is enveloped
in voluptuously textured smoke and shadow—
a veritable spectrum of grays—charcoal, slate,
lead, iron, steel, pewter, pearl, silver, dappled
dove, and ash.

     Only a few brilliant accents bring
the somber composition to life: the crimson
and purple robes of the figures in the Temple
of Concord; scarlet rockets that burst and disperse
"parcels of flame";

     and against the invisible
horizon, a radiant sheet of gold that seems
calculated to set off the silhouette of
the seven-story pagoda: a delicate
skeleton about to come unstrung and tumble.

On the Graphic Representation of Time

Most artists charged by official commission with
documenting major displays of fireworks fix
on the often conflated, often completely
imaginary instant when the great pageant
is at its height,

     all the advertised explosions
blossoming stereotypically against
thickly inked night. Although appropriate fare for
a fête book, such fanciful simplifications

omit too much. More scrupulous
                              draughtsmen, intent
on capturing the actual   precarious
event in its entirety,   must find a means
of incorporating both "before"   and "after"
in a single image. One
                    classic solution
was the diagrammatical   tableau: the whole
festive sequence compressed and unfolding   piecemeal,
its episodes   distributed about the page
as if simultaneous.
                         Contemporary
viewers, versed   in such strategies, would readily
read these discrete scenes   as chapters of a story:
here the insolent   infidels' florid silken
tent is set alight;
                    here our indomitable
infantry defile,   each ensign's insignia
legible. On this litter,   the most holy Host
is conveyed through the clean-swept   cathedral square, where
tumblers with balance
                         beams are capering above
the upturned heads   of revelers at heavily
laden festal boards;   a ship of fools is scuttled
amid applause; a frightened horse   rears and throws its
rider when the pyre ignites;
                              now a hellmouth roars
and belches flame, and, almost   at the margin, half-
hidden behind   the battlements, the climactic
feu de joie appears as just   a few asterisks
trailing broken trajectories.
                         The twenty-first-
century eye may   be disoriented by
this synchronous omnibus format.   We prefer

a two-tiered approach in which   day and night are not
superimposed.
                        At the bottom, orderly rows
of unspent matériel   (girandoles loaded
with grenades, Roman candles,   cannons, Catherine
wheels) are all labeled   alphabetically, keyed
to a neatly printed table.
                             Each object (but
not its indexical letter)   casts a small, sharp
shadow on the otherwise   empty parade ground.
Above it, where we would expect a sky,   a sky,
but as blank as the bleached, raked sand
                                  and abruptly
abbreviated. Instead   of the midday sun,
we see a darkened duplicate   scene descending
like a window shade.   The wicks are lit; fireworks scratch
their flourishes across a
                        full-scale firmament.
Curiously, this glorious   finale fails
to hold our full attention.   Once we adjust to
the tight cross-hatching that signifies   night, our eyes
tend to slide
                  down the umbilical trail linking
each of the exuberant   freeze-frame conclusions
to the scorched patch of earth where it started,   then jump
back to the overilluminated   boxed list
to locate its name. Or else
                        we may shrink away
from the "fine frenzy"   and squint through thickets of smoke
until we think   we see the pyrotechnician
hurrying from fuse to fuse,   brandishing his bunch
of gray touch papers and his white-tipped   stick of punk.

ON THE METAPHORIC IMPULSE

Chrysanthemums, umbrellas,   sno-cones, colonies
of polyps, mops, plumes,   harpoons, spermatozoa,
milkweed seeds: we seem to be   unable to see
fireworks without transforming their

                                   drifting, swiftly
disintegrating   configurations of sparks
into images.   Starting with Aristotle,
many have remarked   on the human tendency
to discover or invent

                        likenesses, even
(or especially) in the most   unlike objects,
"to give the thing   a name that belongs to something
else." Numerous   attempts have been made to explain
this trait.

                  Perhaps the propensity to equate
disparate phenomena   conferred a certain
selective advantage on   those hominids with
a penchant for tropes,   whether because they amused
potential mates

                      (a tenuous hypothesis),
or because metaphorical   thinking signals
greater overall   cognitive capacity,
which naturally   translates into a crucial
competitive edge.

                  This latter conjecture, while
more plausible,   is equally impossible
to verify; therefore we   must reluctantly
limit ourselves to a lesser   question we can
better address:

                  How does our taste in imagery
vary, vacillate,   or even evolve over
time and space?   With reference to fireworks, we observe

that the displays themselves remain   essentially
unchanged down through the centuries;

                           nevertheless,
their graphic representations   are constantly
finding new forms—   from the biomorphic (twining
intestines, thistles, sheaves of wheat),   to the martial
(the tassels on shakos, spiked mace heads,

                           mushroom clouds),
to the domestic   (brushes, feather dusters, lace
curtains, spurting shower nozzles).   Do these diverse
metaphors in fact   reflect characteristics
of their respective eras?

                   When we trace spindly
white rocket trails   across the medieval sky,
and see a mycelium   threading through the loam,
its multiple fruiting tips   erupting in spores,
or maggots eating their way

                        out of cheese, are these
analogies the artists'   or our own? Unless
the creator happens to have left   a statement
(which is rarely the case), all   our speculations
are idle, and if

              the fluted columns of flame
celebrating the birth of a late   Louis look
as though they were crowned   with crumbling Corinthian
capitals, and their upright   symmetrical lines
remind us of

             the sand-blasted alabaster
façades of ancient temples,   this may well be mere
retrospective projection.   We thus must further
restrict our scope   to the only subject we may
realistically hope

           to describe: ourselves.
Which visual similes seem   aptest to us?

Next to no   non-anecdotal data have been
gathered on whether   or not we agree about
what resembles what.

                                This is where we should begin.
Returning again   to fireworks, let us focus
on the unstable   constellations we persist
in imposing upon them.   When we see either
an actual
                    pyrotechnical spectacle
or a pictorial record   (mediated
but durable),   let us study our impressions
rigorously, reading the   scribbled-upon sky
as a sort of Rorschach blot, or
                                a message flashed
at us by an old mirror that   has lost almost
all its silvering.   After we identify
the shapes we make   out of the brilliant particles
scattering into the dark,   we can turn to why.

On the Conflation of Opposite Elements

A giant jellyfish hovers   above a church
in Renaissance Rome;   the solemn celebration
of an imperial wedding   at Notre Dame
is enlivened   by undulating streamers
of seaweed;
                    even the opening of the Great
New York and Brooklyn   Bridge is illuminated
by a burning   flotilla of vermilion, gold,
and crimson cephalopods,   whose incandescent
bulbs have commandeered the heavens.
                                If we study
four centuries' worth   of depictions of fireworks,

we may wonder why, amidst   all the incessant
fluctuations in graphic   styles and conventions,
one theme persists:

        the sky as sea, and the fleeting
flames as sea creatures—at first glance,   an odd, even
oxymoronic metaphor.   Why should an artist
interpret a tableau of fire   in air in terms
of flesh in water?

        Some scholars choose to construe
our affinity   for aquatic imagery
as atavistic,   a reflection of our own
marine origins.   An intriguing conjecture,
but far-fetched.

        Surely a simpler solution lies
in actual parallels: fluid movement through
black or blue   depths or heights, inhospitable to
human intruders.   When we peer awkwardly up
or down from our safe, pedestrian

        middle ground,
we are often momentarily   unanchored,
vertiginous;   and thus the antithetical,
rarefied regions   and their boneless denizens
resolve for us into one.

        A monarch's emblem
carved out of the dark   in white fire effervesces
like the crest of a breaker   and then is absorbed
by the implacable background;   a fuse catches,
and we hear the hiss

        of spent waves dissipating
into foam on sand.   A volley of squibs? A school
of small fry flashing   by, bioluminescing
in distress. A bigger squall   is brewing, so we
hold our breath.

        The current is pulling us farther

out to sea. What will we find there?   Starfish, of course.
Coral gardens   and dense clusters of celestial
anemones, their many   oral arms outstretched
in welcome, then wilting away.
                                        Another surge.
At the peak, a plump, unkempt   medusa pulses,
and, like some submarine Rapunzel,   lets fall all
her long, loose, glistening coils.   The lack of landmarks
in this new vista, and its
                              mutability,
distort our sense of distance.   When we try to touch
the oscillating tresses,   we find our fingers
clutching at nothing.   Somewhere where the horizon
might once have been,
                              slender tentacles still beckon
with venomous tips.   In answer, an armada
of man-of-wars advances, a vast   host, massed for
one final struggle. Our field   of vision is filled
with glowing, semitransparent
                                        multiple lobes.
A wind ripples their margins.   The radiance swells
until the suspended bells   burst in a chorus
of flying fire.   The tentatively sketched figure
dissolves, and the descending sparks
                                        are extinguished.
The show is over. The black scrim   hangs flat again,
and deep overhead,   one last, late quicksilver squid
squirts itself out   of reach, leaving its openmouthed
would-be pursuers blinking   in a puff of ink.

Medusa Beach

ACKNOWLEDGMENTS

Thanks to Fales Library at New York University, where I was able to examine first editions of H.D. and Wyndham Lewis. (In both the 1918 and the 1928 editions of *Tarr*, the word in question is *jellyish*, not *jellyfish*.) Thanks to Thomas Bach, for his help before, during, and after my visit to the Villa Medusa; to Eva Hayward for alerting me to relevant work by Mark Doty and H.D.; and to Victoria Miguel for telling me about "The Adventure of the Lion's Mane."

NOTE ON SOURCES

A great deal of the material in this poem is taken from published sources. When I have borrowed a single word, I've put it in italics; longer borrowings are in quotation marks. In addition to the identified quotes and the many snippets of Matthew Arnold's "Dover Beach," I have included words and phrases from poems by Elizabeth Bishop, Byron, Dickinson, W. S. Gilbert, W. E. Henley, Oliver Wendell Holmes, Homer, Hopkins, Lear, Pound, Rimbaud, Shakespeare, Stevens, Tennyson (particularly "The Lotos-Eaters"), Whitman, Wordsworth, and Yeats, and from Virginia Woolf's essay "An Elizabethan Play." The main prose sources for the poem are Robert Richards's erudite and eloquent biography of Ernst Haeckel, and Marjorie Garber and Nancy J. Vickers's fascinating anthology of works on the Medusa theme from antiquity to the present; when I have cited authors from that work at length, I've named them in the text and listed them in the bibliography, along with other sources of general information and brief quotes.

The ocean attracts humans.   You pay top dollar for the room
with the simplest but most mutable view: one line—a sometimes
sharp, sometimes nearly invisible horizon—   and two
planes of restless color: blue, black, gray, green.   Abetted by
sun, moon and wind, the fickle sky,   and what Stevens calls the "machine
of ocean" (now *perplexed*,   now *tense*, *tranced*, *dry*, *obese*), ceaselessly
churn out "fresh transfigurings."

                                 And the humans are transfixed;
even in winter, they park along the shore,   unwrap sandwiches,
and watch the water while they eat.   Sometimes they read or sleep,
lulled by the "tremulous cadence slow"   of the reliable waves,
giving and taking away.   The steadily reiterated
absence of a steady state   is oddly calming; Arnold's
"melancholy, long, withdrawing roar"   makes for a pleasantly plangent
soundtrack to lunch.

                   Then when summer rolls around again, the people
come out of their shells   and swarm along the margins of the deep.
The sand is soft; the ocean laps close by,   "diffusing balm."
You bask on the beach   till the heat starts to hurt, then retreat
into the soothing amniotic swells.   It's idyllic unless
you meet a jellyfish.   You're lolling weightless, serene, thoughts adrift
amidst the infinite. . . . Ocean as echo   of heaven, heartbeat,
fons et origo, "the turbid ebb and flow. . . ."

                                   Out of the blue,
a slab of mucus slaps you in the face.   You jerk your head up
and crawl, stiff-necked and awkward, fast as you can,   back to dry land.
But watch your step;   some of them have come ashore—there's one,
   right there,
glistening stickily like a broken,   yolkless egg, all naked
interior. It's not that you're scared   of being stung; in fact,
you'd almost prefer a sting   to the gentle, accidental
touch of such a flayed, defenseless animal.

                                        Kick the thing
back where it belongs, or bury it in sand.   Or call the kids;
they'll be happy to grab it and run   squealing into the surf.
If no one stops them, they'll toss it around,   dissect it with a stick,
hack it to a pulp with a plastic shovel.   The alien
is routed, for now (but what if each piece   has a life of its own
like the sorcerer's apprentice's broom?),   and order restored
to the seaside summer realm.

                              Back then, the beach was lotos-land,
the opposite of school,   "always afternoon...languid air...sweetened
with the summer light...a half-dream...."   But real: someone sighted
a shark last week.   The silver minnows tickling at your feet
are eating your dead skin.   A sand dollar is a skeleton,
and the breakers could break your neck;   even when you ride them right,
they rake you over the shoals.   Covered with scratches and bites,
sunburned and shivering, the kids begged to stay.

                                                    "Let us alone.
Time driveth onward fast."   Ten more minutes. Five. One more dive
into the chivying tide, one last doomed castle,   then surrender
to the dull, dry everyday.   But there was still one getaway:
you "plunged into a sea of words   and came up dripping": *wine-dark*,
whelming, ructive, whale-road,   multitudinous, sunless, shroud,
mackerel-crowded, gong-tormented,   soundless, sounding, bound-
   less, bounding,
slopping, sultry, syllabub.

                        "There is no Frigate like a Book."
Marooned, you jumped   for whatever tipsy skiff drifted past,
and pushed off into "the sea of stories,"   stories of the sea,
each teaching its lesson: a disobedient   prophet or puppet
will be swallowed by a whale, then saved.   Every island and rock
is a trap, where monsters and women   are waiting to waylay
the homeward-bound hero.   Half-mad old men must battle vast
allegorical foes.

You learned to scan the burnished surface
for irregular ripples, glints, hints   of something big beneath.
The secret is down there but it won't stay put.   You trained for years,
diving deeper, holding your breath   longer. Again and again
you grappled with Proteus;   the sea-god turned into a lion,
a serpent, a pig, a waterfall,   a pillar of flame, a tree,
and you could never hang on long enough   to force him to reveal
his real form, and answer your questions:

Why are the bees dying?
What's happened to all my old friends?   Why am I stuck in the doldrums?
What power have I offended,   and how can I make amends?
No answer. Your words sink, bathetic,   and the waves just thunder on
unintelligibly.   But maybe it's all for the best.
"Human kind," as T. S. Eliot   sententiously observed, "cannot
bear very much reality."   We squeamishly try to evade
what De Casseres calls "Medusa-Truth."

Wicked stepmother
to Proteus, and dam   of Pegasus, the poet's wingèd steed,
Medusa was   (depending on whose story you believe)
Poseidon's lover or his victim,   an African warrior,
a virgin queen, one of three   hideous gorgon sisters, or
a maiden who angered Athena either   by boasting that she
was fairer than the goddess   or by succumbing to "filthy lust"
in the Temple of Wisdom.

Athena turned her flowing hair
to snakes and made her face   too awful to behold. Since then,
she has served as a versatile symbol;   over the centuries,
the exegetes have seen in her   (using their shields as mirrors)
a potent force for good   and/or evil, "the epitome
of the apotropaic object."   Euripides describes
a locket holding two drops of her blood: "One is poisonous,
the other cures disease."

She has been equated with the sun,
"the tempestuous loveliness   of terror," tyranny,
revolution, the colonized nation,   the Jew, the body,
death, pleasure, the Other,   the Self made paralyzingly
self-aware by the awareness   of another's gaze,
and so forth.   For Marx she is the misery engendered
by capitalism, facts from which   we avert our eyes
in selfish denial.

Most common are readings of the gorgon
as what Neumann says "we might justly call   'the Infernal Feminine,'"
her "gnashing mouth" and gaping neck   as "the devouring chasm
of the uroboric womb."   Freud finds in her "a confirmation
of the technical rule   according to which a multiplication
of penis symbols signifies castration."   Luckily, her gift
for petrifying men   means that penis loss is somehow
accompanied by a "comforting erection."

Some view this
"phallic woman" as a modern   phenomenon (for Benjamin
she is "the face of modernity itself")   and the destroyer
of the modern male.   Wylie says she is "the perfidious
materialism of mom . . .   the dynasty of the dames,"
the dark, secret side of the blond   Cinderella ideal:
"ruby lips case-hardened into pliers   for bending males like wire,"
turning them "not to stone, but to slime."

Often she is linked
with "oratory, an art   which, by changing men's desires,
erases their former thought";   her coiling locks are "rhetorical
ornament," "the power   of the letter to enthrall."   She thus
represents "an interpretive as well   as a moral threat,"
both the awful truth and the attempt   to suppress it.   Nietzsche says:
"Great thought is like Medusa's head: all the world's features harden,
a deadly, ice-cold battle."

Jack London, in *The Mutiny
of the Elsinore,*   quotes De Casseres, "the American
Nietzsche," on the "war   against the truth; that is, against the
Real."
Man "shuns facts from his infancy.   His life is a perpetual
evasion. Miracle,   chimera and tomorrow keep him alive.
He lives on fiction and myth. It is the lie   that makes him free. . . .
Hope, Belief, Fable,   Art, God, Socialism, Immortality,
Alcohol, Love."
    The foolhardy adventurer who dares
to look directly at Medusa   will be paralyzed
by the mesmerizing writhing   of her "viperine hair"
and by his own visceral revulsion   at her empty eyes
and her "wide-open mouth   with the lolling tongue," an emblem,
according to De Casseres,   of the mortal, material
meaninglessness of the modern world.   The "Don Juan of knowledge,"
warns Nietzsche, will become "a guest of stone."

                                                    Both primordial
and modern, the gorgon is always a danger.   In London's "last
great effort," "The Red One," Bassett,   a naturalist, is lured
by a "melting sweet" music   deep into the bush, the taboo
interior of Guadalcanal.   His native guide, "his queer
little monkey face eloquent with fear,"   refuses to go on.
("That big fella noise no good,   all same devil-devil.")
He runs off, and Bassett soon

                            stumbles upon his headless corpse.
The savages attack; Bassett flees   and struggles for days or weeks
through a "dank and noisome jungle"   which "actually stank with evil."
Near death, he is rescued by Baletta,   who regards him "with peering
querulous eyes that blinked   as blinked the eyes of denizens
of monkey-cages."   "At first she had squealed in delight at the sight
of his helplessness   and was for bashing his brains out
with a stout branch."

But enchanted by his "pristine whiteness,"
she brings him to Ngurn, the medicine man,   and Bassett recovers
in a hut festooned with shrunken heads.   Ngurn tells him the music comes
from "The Thunderer," "The Red One," "The Star-Born."   More he
    will not say.
To learn the tribal secret, Bassett must   master his disgust
and woo Baletta. At his caress,   she "gibbered and squealed
little queer, piglike gurgly   noises of delight." Smitten,
she can refuse him nothing.

                    "She led him into the forbidden
quadrant...a gloomy gorge...a naked mesa...   a tremendous pit...
carpeted with human bones"—   and rising from the pit's deep center,
a huge red pearl   made of some alien substance. "He moved
his fingertips   and felt the whole gigantic sphere quicken and live
and respond...quiver   under the finger-tip caress in rhythmic
vibrations that became...   mutterings of sound...like a peal
from some bell of the gods

                    reaching earthward from across space."
How had this sound   penetrated the depths of the jungle?
"A great king-post...like a battering-ram"   served as a striker,
sending "the voice of God"   into the wilderness, "seducing and
commanding to be heard."   They return to the village, where fever
and Baletta's importunate ardor   leave Bassett so ill
he knows his time is running out.   Ngurn has always been eager
to add a rare white head to his collection.

                    Bassett agrees
to sacrifice his life for one final   encounter with "The God-Voiced."
The natives take him on a "lurching litter"   back through the forest
to the sacred pit where the Red One gleams.   The king-post is released,
and Bassett is "lost in ecstasy."   "Just ere the edge of steel
bit the flesh and nerves,"   he has "a sense of impending marvel
of the rending of walls   before the unimaginable," and sees
"the serene face of the Medusa, Truth."

                                    A century
after the story was published,   its uncomfortable subtext
seems embarrassingly inescapable: Baletta's "grotesque
female hideousness,"   "her rancid-oily and kinky hair"
are more than the "fastidious" Bassett can bear.   The modern male
tries to achieve enlightenment   and escape the "prototype
of woman," but ends up dead, his head   severed, shrunk, and "suspended
from the rafters" as a ghastly trophy.

                                    The Greek myth ended
with a happier decapitation;   many gods joined forces
to help "a 'sacred man'"   slay the terrible "paragon
of all women." Wearing Hades' "helm of darkness,"   Perseus crept,
invisible, into the gorgons' lair,   where Medusa slept,
serpents "draped like a curtain   over her face." He fixed his eyes
on the reflection in Athena's shield,   unsheathed Zeus's sword,
and swung blindly at the source of the image.

                                              Connection,
a hissing scream, resistance, release,   then a thud as the squirming
head hit the ground.   He stuffed it into the pouch provided
by the Hesperides, and clicked his heels.   Hermes' wingèd sandals
bore him safely away, but as he flew   (or so one version
of the story goes),   gorgon blood leaked from the bag and dripped,
like deadly seed, into the sea.   And from each drop arose
a tendril of flesh—a polyp—

                                    that took root in the ocean bed,
where it still branches and spreads.   Scientists confirm that colonies
of polyps may "blanket large expanses   of the ocean floor,"
swaying like poppies in the benthic breeze,   and now and then spawning,
possibly in unison,   in an asexual process
called *strobilation*, budding off   crop after crop after crop
of free-swimming *ephyrae*   like infinitesimal, fringed
contact lenses.

Each miniature *medusa* matures
into a capsule of elastic gel   with an "inward-
facing stomach skin"   and sexual organs. It now
reproduces again,   releasing eggs and sperm that meet
and create new *medusae*. The cycle   seems to continue
"indefinitely, effectively   rendering the jellyfish
immortal." Most adults "live for   a few months; however,
the polyp stage may be perennial."

(This could be the source
of the legend, reported in *Gilgamesh*,   that the secret
of eternal life lies deep in the ocean.   For many years,
the process perplexed naturalists,   especially since most types
of polyps make only more polyps.   It was like a case
of "a caterpillar turning into   either another
caterpillar, or   a butterfly, and of butterflies
producing butterflies.")

Ensnaring prey in its complex frill
of oral arms and tentacles,   the young jellyfish feeds and grows.
(Most common northern species reach   the size of a salad plate.)
The *medusa*'s radial   symmetry "allows it to detect
and respond to food or danger   from any direction."
It propels itself   by expanding and contracting the muscular
margins of its bell,   and when the tide and temperature are right,
washes up on your beach.

No! Not again! Get that disgusting myth
away from my towel!   You turn your back, collect some pretty shells,
and think about easier creatures: the shorebirds (their wings
make them ideal for wishful musings)   or mammals like us:
the whales in their hidden grandeur   singing across the abyss,
the porpoises that sport   like puppies in our wake, the seals
who meet our gaze   with friendly curiosity, as if
eager to play.

When humans trawl the deep for totems, they select
those with faces or behaviors   onto which they can project
their own: the skittish hermit crab, holed up in its stolen home,
the clownishly flopping and flailing octopus,   the dead-eyed shark
with its inexhaustible,   advancing batallions of teeth.
Or the chambered nautilus,   the solitary artist,
that spends its life in "silent toil,"   constructing its "ship of pearl."
"Build thee more stately mansions, O my soul!"

                                           The jellyfish
offers no drama, no comedy, no uplift.   You have trouble
seeing a reflection of yourself   in an organism
that has no brain, no eyes, no limbs   (unless you count the dangling
    clump
of oral arms) and just one opening   for both mouth and anus.
Behind glass, at the aquarium,   they are pleasingly
abstract—pure protean   form, color, and rhythm—"floating
lingerie" or "living lava lamps."

                              Only poets,
the most self-absorbed   of human subspecies, read these
animated Rorschach blots   as figures for their own
mental processes,   and they, too, keep the jellyfish itself
at arm's length. Even Moore,   laureate of the unlovely,
although she admires   the *medusa*'s elusiveness,
doesn't approach very close before   abandoning it
as untouchable.

                         Most poets start with real *medusae*, but
quickly convert them into something else.   When Plath goes boating
and passes through a swarm of jellyfish,   "pushing by like hearts,
Red stigmata at the very center... a placenta,"
she thinks of her gorgon mother: "Your wishes   Hiss at my sins.
Off, off, eely tentacle!"   Clampitt waxes homiletic:
"ay, in the very tissue of desire   lodge viscid barbs that turn
the blood to coral."

Doty sees jellyfish as metaphors
for metaphors, "nothing but trope . . . nothing but style."   He compares
a pulsing jellyfish bell   to a mouth forming words—an image
one could easily extend: an insatiable maw that sucks in
every passing particle   of experience, then spews
the digested residue.   As usual, the poet
hurries back from the external world   to his own cozy
brain and its products.
                          Weighted down with referential ballast
and florid verbiage, the actual animal   sinks out of sight.
Although some jellyfish can grow   longer than a blue whale,
and masses of *medusae* have caused   panic and near-disaster
by clogging the cooling systems   of nuclear reactors,
they do not figure   as terrifying adversaries
in nautical thrillers   or metaphysical epics; they still
await their Melville.
                      The few medusoid creatures that appear
in fiction are most often   like Lovecraft's "floating horrors":
a "gelatinous green immensity,"   or the "sticky spawn
of the stars," which has arrived on a meteor   from some hideous
non-Euclidean world, and is worshipped   by "swarthy cult fiends."
These "unhallowed blasphemies . . . dream beneath the sea,"   biding
   their time,
surfacing only occasionally   to swallow a boat, or
engulf an empire.
                  The "things which cannot be mentioned"
are apparently invulnerable.   When a "brave Norwegian"
"drove his vessel head-on   against the pursuing jelly, which rose
above the unclean froth   like the stern of a demon galleon,"
he saw, in the "venomous seething"   and the "stench as of a thousand
opened graves," that "God in heaven!—   the scattered plasticity
of that nameless   sky-spawn was nebulously *recombining*
in its hateful original form."

There is no escaping
its "flabby claws."   Whoever witnesses "that riot
of luminous amorphousness"   is doomed to madness or "grey
brittle death."   As one victim says, "It feeds on everything livin'
an' gits stronger all the time."   Such tales tend to end with portentous,
scriptural predictions: "What has risen may sink, and what has sunk
may rise. Loathsomeness waits   and dreams in the deep, and decay
spreads over the tottering cities of men."

In fact, such visions
resemble the recent real-life global   "jellyfish explosion."
"Anthropogenic stressors"   such as eutrophication,
overfishing, and rising temperatures   have led to conditions
far more favorable   to jellyfish than to other
marine species. Seed colonies   of *medusae* hitch rides
in ballast water; we transport them   thousands of miles. They thrive
and multiply, worldwide.

"Fishermen in the Gulf of Mexico
complain of jellyfish blooms   so thick you can walk across
the water on them," and "off the coast   of Florida, Spain,
Italy and Japan, a growing fleet   of unrecognized,
invasive invertebrates   is floating silently, almost
invisible, a thin skin   flexing with the waves and tides
that animate all the ocean."   The whole marine system
"has been reorganized."

Moreover, a few *medusa* species,
like unkillable sci-fi creatures,   may really be immortal.
Turritopsis undergoes   the standard metamorphosis
from polyp to mature *medusa*, but   in "response to adverse
conditions, including senescence,"   it regresses. The bell
everts; the tentacles degenerate.   No longer able
to swim, it settles onto a substrate,   where it can wait
indefinitely for better times.

(This is not the "cruel immortality" of the bard Tithonis,   who begged his divine lover, the Dawn, for eternal life,   but forgot to request eternal youth as well.   First his lips, then his tongue, then all the rest of his flesh shriveled away;   he became a cicada, and each morning he still greets his beloved,   pulsing his stiff exoskeletal tymbals   as she passes overhead, always radiant and fresh.

Tennyson tells how he suffered, doomed forever to remember how he too   had once been young, felt his "blood glow," and basked   in her caress: "Mouth, forehead, eyelids growing dewy-warm,   With kisses balmier than half-opening buds." But how the Dawn felt   when she found him waiting for her every day, a little smaller and drier,   but rasping out the same aubade, is an element of the plot   that has been lost in the course of millennia of not-

always-flawless transmission. Tithonis says she wept dewy tears,   as she brushed his brittle cheek with her rosy fingers.   Did it break her immortal heart to watch her lover wither   into "a white-haired shadow"? Or was the dew just dew,   and did his pathetic, desiccated stridulations annoy her?   Why couldn't the goddess have granted the missing wish unasked?   Could the lapse have been deliberate, revenge for some unrecorded offense?)

In their seminal paper, Piraino, Boero,   Aeschbach, and Schmid bluntly state that in nonmodular   organisms, "the onset of sexual reproduction   ultimately leads to death." But *Turritopsis* avoids this fate.   Its mature, specialized cells transdifferentiate and become   totipotent again, "like a chicken that transforms   into an egg that gives birth to another chicken."

The mechanism is a mystery.
Needless to say,   scientists are striving to understand how
Turritopsis reverses   the ontogenetic process
that, for us, goes just one way.   Humans and jellyfish are nearly
identical genetically, so   these findings could well have
enormous repercussions.   They may also inspire
more serious literature,   elevating the jellyfish out
of the pulp-fiction ghetto.

Thus far, the *medusa*'s greatest claim
to literary fame   has been "The Adventure of the Lion's Mane."
Sherlock Holmes's peaceful seaside retirement   is interrupted when
a half-dressed man staggers up from the beach   and dies in agonized
paroxysms, his torso aflame   with "long, angry weals,"
as if he had been scourged.   A note "in a scrawling feminine hand"
leads to Maud,   his secret love, "the beauty of the neighborhood...
wide-eyed and intense."

Holmes says, "I could not look upon her
without realizing that no young man   would cross her path unscathed."
Suspicion falls on a rejected suitor   whose "coal-black eyes
and swarthy face" suggest "some outlandish blood."   But then he, too,
is attacked while bathing! Now Holmes understands.   Both men
    have fallen
into the deadly embrace   of the lion's mane jellyfish.
Its venom races   straight to the heart, and those who touch it perish
in "exquisite torment."

He leads the baffled Inspector
to the tide pool where the victims swam,   and points to "a curious
waving, vibrating hairy creature   with streaks of silver
among its yellow tresses.   It pulsated with a slow, heavy
dilation and contraction."   Perhaps a storm has washed it in,
since, as the Inspector says, "It don't belong   to Sussex." They crush it
with a boulder; "a thick, oily scum   oozed out from below
the stone and stained the water round." Case closed.

This queasy, quasi-
lubricious focus   on certain suggestive features
of *medusa* physiology   can also be observed
in the largest popular genre   of jellyfish literature:
books for young children, who   revel in the slimy and the mildly
taboo: *Ooey-Gooey   Animals, Jellyfish Jam, Wee
on a Jellyfish Sting and Other Lies   That Grown-Ups Tell You,
Boogers of the Sea.*
                    Scientists, the primary adult
readers and writers of jellyfish books,   do not react
to unfamiliar anatomy   with squeamish glee; they are drawn
to the same alien   features that repel the layman:
transparency ("guts and gonads   on display for anyone to see")
and placid, efficient voracity   ("like swimming mouths," massed
in millions beneath the surface,   "sweeping the water clean
of every small living thing").
                    Biologists admire success,
and jellyfish have triumphed everywhere.   "From pole to pole
and around the equator,   in shallow waters and the ocean depths,
we find jellies in nearly every niche,"   absorbing nourishment
as their "gentle jets"   spurt them along in "quivering
peristaltic waves,"   each species with its own distinctive rhythm.
"It is heartening to know   that you can still be elegant
without a brain reflex."
                    While many are concerned about "large-scale
disruption to pelagic   ecosystems" and the prospect
of a *medusa* monoculture,   they often find a bright side.
"The Jellyfish Joyride: Causes, Consequences and Management
Responses to a More Gelatinous Future"   cites evidence
that jellyfish alleviate   "arthritis, bronchitis, burns,
fatigue, gout, hypertension,   menstruation pain and ulcers."
They are also an excellent source of protein.

But scientists
write mainly for other scientists.   Their taxonomies
(*Monograph of the British   Naked-Eye Medusae
with Figures of All the Species*)   and practical studies
("The Energy Density   of Jellyfish: Estimates
from Bomb-Calorimetry   and Proximate-Composition"),
however important,   tend to be incomprehensible
to nonspecialist readers.
                            The book that has done the most
to enhance the jellyfish's   popular appeal
is Ernst Haeckel's 1904 bestseller,   *Art Forms in Nature*.
Its hundred morphological tableaux   (still widely reproduced)
depict in dizzyingly   meticulous decorative detail
a vast array of living beings: blastoids,   single-celled
radiolarians,   algae, sponges, and fungi, as well
as a few vertebrates.
                            Almost twenty percent of the plates
are devoted to Haeckel's favorites: the "splendid *medusae*,"
and to their simple polyp and   colonial relatives.
The varied regularities   of their harmonious forms
perfectly serve his purpose: to display for the delight
and education of the general public   the seemingly
limitless symmetries   that he discovered governing
every level of life.
                            Water was Haeckel's element.
Bölsche, his first biographer,   describes the "magical summer"
when the young medical student   was introduced to the ocean
by his anatomy professor, Müller.   Every morning
they rowed along the coast   of the remote archipelago
of Heligoland,   trailing modified butterfly nets,
then spent the afternoons examining   their "pelagic sweepings"
under microscopes.

Each drop was teeming with fantastic beings—
transparent, iridescent—an incredibly   "beautiful medley"
of life-forms, "a Noah's ark   in the space of a pinch of snuff."
Haeckel wrote to his parents   that he was "under a spell."
He "turned himself   into a marine mammal, living half
in the water for days together."   The bemused locals called him
a "sea-devil." He soon gave up medicine   for zoology
and "the fairyland of the sea."

But Haeckel's life was not charmed.
His adored wife, Anna Sethe,   died on his thirtieth birthday,
and he went "mad with grief,"   delirious, slipping in and out
of consciousness for over a week.   When he was out of danger,
his parents sent him to Nice,   hoping that the sea would help him heal,
but his modern biographer, Richards,   records that thereafter
he spent every birthday alone.   "He could not work, could not eat,
and often tempted himself with death."

Already a skeptic,
he now lost the last vestiges   of religious belief.
He rejected the consoling notion   of an immortal soul,
taking comfort instead   in the beauty of Nature, and the hope
that man would one day come to understand   her universal laws.
Zoological research was thus "a cause   that might transcend
individual fragility. . . .   For Haeckel, love fled
and hid her face among sea creatures."

The Mediterranean
did soothe him. He found new   species of beautiful *medusae*.
The "most charming . . . a magical sight,"   floating alone in a tide pool,
seemed to him a living vision   of his Anna. "I enjoyed
several happy hours   watching the play of her tentacles,
which hung like blond hair-ornaments   from the delicate
umbrella-cap, and which with the softest   movement would roll up
into thick, short spirals."

　　　　　　　　　　　　　　　He named it *Mitrocoma annae*,
"Anna's headband, the princess　　of the Eucopiden," and when,
years later, he discovered another,　　"even lovelier"
new species, he called it　　*Desmonema annasethe*. It, too,
seemed "to embody the spirit of his 'true　　unforgettable wife.'"
(Richards drily notes　　that Haeckel wrote these tender words
when he had been married for twelve years　　"to his apparently
forgettable second wife, Agnes.")
　　　　　　　　　　　　　　　Haeckel was the last
of the classical　　*Naturphilosophen*, both zoologist
and artist, "apostle　　of the gospel of Goethe"
and ardent Darwinian.　　Unlike Arnold, he was not dismayed
at the ebbing of the "Sea of Faith";　　he eagerly stripped off
"the variegated clothing　　of the God idea," to unveil
nature's true nature,　　and saw the "naked shingles of the world"
as covered with treasure.
　　　　　　　　　　　　　　Striving to undo the dualists'
divorce of mind from matter,　　he argued that, since every atom
was endowed with the powers　　of repulsion and attraction,
it was thus, in a sense, "ensouled,"　　and he founded the Monist League
to fight for an end　　to such "homotheistic" superstitions
as an anthropomorphic god,　　personal survival
after death, and free will,　　which were "purely the product
of poetic imagination."
　　　　　　　　　　　　　But Haeckel was not opposed
to poetry; he found　　"great pleasure and consolation"
in Goethe, Schiller, and Shakespeare.　　"Poetry raises a man
above the dust and worry　　of everyday life and banishes
evil thoughts."　　Imagination, as his teacher Müller said,
is not the enemy of wisdom,　　but "an indispensable
servant...that fills up the gaps　　left by the intelligence in our
knowledge of the connections of things."

Both good Humboldtians,
they believed that observation   can be "scientifically exact
without being evacuated   of the vivifying breath
of imagination. The poetic   character must derive
from the intuited connection   between the sensuous
and the intellectual, from the feeling   of the vastness
and of the mutual   limitation and unity
of living nature."
                              Arnold shuddered and turned away
from his water-view window,   back to his bride and his warm,
safe chamber. But for Haeckel,   even in his bereavement,
the godless universe was not all dismal   "struggle and flight";
it was a "highly developed crystal,"   each of whose myriad
facets ("so various,   so beautiful, so new") would disclose
part of the unified natural law   to anyone who dared
look closely at the facts.
                              In 1867, when Arnold
published "Dover Beach,"   Haeckel was plunging, in exuberant
pursuit of *medusae*, into   the "great animal soup"
off Tenerife,   and for the next fifty years, he returned,
whenever he could, to the sea: Corsica, Tunis, Lisbon,
Sumatra, Singapore.... His *Visit to Ceylon* records
"how he greeted his beloved   *medusae* in their magnificent
tropical form."
                              He bottled specimens and brought them back
to landlocked Jena, where he taught,   and built a "Temple
of Monism," his Phyletic Museum,   still the only one
devoted to evolution   and to "the holy trinity"
of Goethean/Spinozan belief,   the three inseparable
"highest ideals of mankind,"   the moral, intellectual,
and aesthetic aspects   of the one all-encompassing Substance:
"the good, the true and the beautiful."

The museum's façade
was embellished with stylized   depictions of plankton,
sea urchins, and jellyfish,   based on Haeckel's drawings
of "art forms from the ocean."   In the entrance hall, a larger-than-life
statue of Truth,   "a glorious virgin, bearing a torch
in her right hand, and in her left   the skull of a chimpanzee,"
invited visitors to inspect   Haeckel's collection and learn
how all living things are connected.

Genealogical trees
delineated degrees   of relatedness, from "monera"
to man. Vitrines of insects,   shells, skeletons, and taxidermied
vertebrates (including some of Darwin's   own finches) displayed
nature's diversity,   and models of fetal mammals,
reptiles, and amphibians   showed how individuals
of various species develop,   passing through phases
that bear witness to their shared ancestry.

In the terse
popular simplification   of Haeckel's most famous statement,
"Ontogeny recapitulates   phylogeny." Embryos
of every species in their amniotic sacs   start out nearly
identical, then gradually diverge,   revealing their "common
descent" from some "hypothetical   organism" that "plied
the ancient seas and gave rise   in the course of time to all
of the multi-celled animals."

Jena became "the citadel
of evolution ... the Mecca   for young zoologists."
But not everyone was grateful   to have the theistic scales
removed from their eyes.   Many resented hearing that their faith
was a delusion, and they found   "the dogma of the ape-man"
a distasteful replacement;   Haeckel's pedagogical crusade
met with stiff resistance,   and he was widely anathematized
for waging "war upon God."

Bölsche reports, "The Philistines
are in arms. The quiet, stubborn group   that has vegetated
unchanged, like a demoralized   parasitic animal,
through thousands of years of the free   development of the mind,
boycotts the professor and his family."   For half his life,
Haeckel was the "arch-heretic" of Europe,   denounced from countless
pulpits, pilloried in the press,   attacked by his colleagues, and shunned
by old teachers and former friends.

Of course, "his own volatile
and combative personality"   further provoked his foes.
He dismissed the Christian deity   as "a gaseous vertebrate,"
and an article   from *The London Telegraph*, headlined
"Haeckel Kills the Soul,"   records a typical response to critics:
"I have been blamed   for saying that the Papacy is the greatest
swindle that ever dominated   the world of thought. I will
substitute the word *humbug* for *swindle*."

Haeckel himself
faced charges of fraud   when a reviewer of his *Natural
History of Creation*   noticed that the illustrations
purporting to show similarities   between the early
embryos of three species   had been printed from a single block.
Haeckel admitted the "formal lapse,"   explaining that he had been
"quite rushed," and the error   was corrected in the next edition.
But the damage was done.

Haeckel's many detractors eagerly
seized on this apparent proof   that he was playing "a game
of three-card monte   with the public and with science." Darwin
and Huxley defended him   (Huxley wrote, "May your shadow
never be less,   and may all your enemies, unbelieving dogs
who resist the Prophet   of Evolution, be deviled
by the sitting of jackasses   upon their grandmothers' graves!"),
but Haeckel was discouraged and depressed.

                                         The ocean again
restored him; he traveled   from the Isle of Jersey to the Red Sea,
compiling material   for his magisterial
two-folio tome,   *System der Medusen*. And on a hill
in Jena, on the "consecrated" spot   where Goethe had made
his famous sketch of Schiller's garden house,   he built a new home,
the Villa Medusa, which would become   "the stable pole
of his turbulent life."
                              Today the Italianate villa
houses the Haeckel archive.   You can see watercolor sketches
from his *Medusa Album*,   a letter from Darwin, an iris
from his schoolboy herbarium,   and a report card that attests
to his "laudable proficiency"   in gym class. A glass case
of first editions is flanked by the halves   of an immense bivalve,
which may once have served as washbasins,   mounted on sinuous
wrought-iron stands.
                              Here is Haeckel, 23, wary-eyed,
posed awkwardly behind   his starched, high-collared parents.
At 47, bandoliered,   in spotless tropical gear,
he holds his rifle and topee in one hand;   from the other
dangles a dead, long-tailed jungle mammal.   On a New Year's card
("a fleeting remembrance of Bayreuth")   he is strolling, in white ducks,
with Isadora Duncan,   who has just composed a dance
in honor of his seventieth birthday.
                              A bronze plaque
commissioned by his students   shows him standing in a rowboat,
apparently bargaining   with a seaweed-festooned Nereid
who has half-emerged from the bay   and is leaning languidly
on his gunwale, offering a large   starfish for his inspection.
In the background, Vesuvius fumes,   and high in the sky,
a celestial chorus line   of six plump, shimmying *medusae*
presides over the scene.

Even here in the house there are
jellyfish overhead.   In the former dining room, you look up
into the eight cerulean and sunset   lobes of a frescoed
Discomedusa's subumbrella;   it rests on its lacy,
tasseled mouth-arms, as if on a bed   of golden acanthus.
A metal cap obscures the mouth and gonads.   From the center,
an electric cord   descends, umbilical, ending
in an elaborate eight-armed candelabrum.

                                    Now you enter
Haeckel's study; his pens,   inkwells, blotter, microscope, and slides,
ready on his desk, would suggest   that he had just stepped out
for a moment, except   for the suspicious tidiness
and the death mask by the empty letter rack.   You inhale the dense
Wilhelmine atmosphere,   submerged in a looking-glass ocean,
where dust motes swim   like protozoans, in and out of thin
rivulets of pale, time-filtered light.

                                Once your eyes adjust,
you notice that you're not alone.   Paintings and busts of scientists,
poets, and other primates   gaze gravely back at the "guest
from the future."   One *Pithecanthropus alalus* (believed
in Haeckel's day to be the missing   link) is grimacing
under the weight   of the tabletop on his head. Another
poses with his wife and child,   a "contented-looking," if hirsute
and prehensile-toed, "burgher family."

                                    And everywhere
you discover more   *medusae*: embroidered on a pillow
on Haeckel's reading chair,   carved into furniture, cast in metal.
A mother-of-pearl   *Desmonema annasethe* drifts across
an intricately inlaid chest,   a gift from the Monist League,
and on the ceiling,   *Periphylla mirabilis* curls her pale
blue-gray tentacles, beckoning seductively.   Even the guls
in the carpet seem to be jellyfish bells.

You hold your breath,
delaying your return   to the terrestrial present.
You want to linger with Haeckel and Bölsche,   deep in your murky
subaqueous prehistory: "Once again, you become what you were,
what your ancestors were. As you 'become,'   that is, as you detach
yourself as an individual   from the huge tree of mankind,
your own development again   tempestuously whizzes
through the whole line from bacillus to man."

                                        Maybe this sense
of contact with some primordial organism   that both is
and isn't you   is what H.D. meant by "jelly-fish consciousness":
a sort of ecstatic receptive state   in which "a set
of super-feelings" emanate   from the brain and the womb,
and "extend out and about us…   part of the super-mind
as the jelly-fish feelers are part   of the jelly-fish itself,
elongated in fine threads."

                              And maybe the jellyfish
is a better model   of how to live in a modern
disenchanted world   than the chambered nautilus, whose "stately
mansions" form a tenement   of brittle cells, "each new temple"
a little   larger than but otherwise identical
to the one before. The "frail tenant"   passes its "dim dreary life"
barricaded inside, and extrudes   its timid tentacles
only to grab at food.

                        Some modernists celebrate armatures.
In 1918, in the inaugural   issue of *Blast*,
Wyndham Lewis extols the striving soul   "perched like aviator
in basin of skull,"   gliding safely above the "thick, sickly
puddle of humanity."   His hero, Arghol, "agon
of the intellect,"   tries to kill off Hanp, his lumpen "half-
disciple" and physical foil,   "an unclean little beast"
who drags him down to "death, anti-manhood."

"Always *à deux*!"

How can "the mind, perverse and gorgeous,"   "the free subject,"
    break away
from the "amphibious sluggish body"?   Lewis recommends
"a mechanizing of the natural,"   a rigorous
"masculine formalism."   In an essay on himself,
he trumpets "*externality*,   in a world that is literally
inundated with sexual viscera   and the 'dark'
gushings of the tides of *The Great Within*."

The skull, the hull,
the helmet, the tank, the church,   and the Vorticist skyscraper
protect the "Classical" artist-hero   from the "great decay,"
"the bog" of the Romantic.   "In contrast to the jellyfish
that floats at the center   of the subterranean
stream of the 'dark' Unconscious,   I much prefer, for my part,
the shell of the tortoise, or   the rigid stylistic
articulations of the grasshopper."

A sturdy verbal
carapace conceals the "impure" core,   the "soft quivering
quick flesh," with its slimy taint   of the feminine, "enemy
of the absolute."   Lewis had his own theory of evolution:
"The masculine is not   the natural human state,
but a carefully nurtured   secondary development
above the normal and womanly."   (Recent evidence on
how unexpectedly common

parthenogenesis is
suggests that Lewis was right, though not quite   in the way he meant.)
Frederick Tarr, the sub-Nietzschean   protagonist of Lewis's
eponymous "aporetic   autocritique" sums up the view:
"There was only one God   and he was a man. A woman was
a lower form of life.   Everything was female to begin with.
A jellyish diffuseness spread itself   and gaped on the beds
and in the bas-fonds of everything."

(Many recent scholars cite this passage slightly differently, replacing this and one other occurrence of the word *jellyish* with *jellyfish*. Although Lewis often mentions jellyfish in later works, this early *medusa* image appears to be apocryphal, a simple transcription error that happened to please the critics and has thus been reproduced, in a process that one might call "textual selection.")

In *Tarr* (which Eliot describes as "civilization criticized... by an orang-outang of genius"), the hero strives to rise above "the slop of sex," although he knows that "everything on the superior side of that line was not purged of jellyish [jellyfish?] attributes." Both Lewis and Tarr are aghast at the growing influence of "the feminine mind" and "deeply feminized" men, too weak for "the perilous Without."

Tarr, whose own intellect is "full of sinister piston-rods, organ-like shapes, heavy drills," blames "giggling invert spinsters" for "a wide and creeping rot in the West," and in *Men Without Art*, Lewis says he feels "very much a fish out of water" in the "suffocating atmosphere" of the "old-maidish" aesthetics and regressive inward focus of Pater, Proust, Wilde, Strachey, Sitwell, Joyce, Stein, James, and Woolf.

Oddly, he approved, at least briefly (presumably swayed by Pound), of H.D. In *Blast*, he cites her "Oread" ("Whirl up Sea— / Whirl your pointed pines / Splash your great pines / On our rocks....") as the poetic equivalent of Picasso or Kandinsky. But a few pages later, he announces that the Vorticists "have mastered the elements.... We have crystallized the sphere into the cube...to express our abstract thoughts of conscious superiority."

From a twenty-first-century standpoint,
that boast seems quaint at best,   and the "proud, handsome
and predatory" externalists less   modern than the adherents
of "the *internal* method" Lewis derides,   less modern even
than Haeckel, who, although he called himself   "wholly a child
of the nineteenth century,"   had already abandoned the view
that man "occupies a special   position in the world
and is separated by a great gulf

                                        from the rest of nature."
Haeckel coined the term *ecology*,   and grasped the central role
of the "one linked sea that covers   two-thirds of the planet"
in sustaining all life.   A recent film on Haeckel, *Proteus:
A Nineteenth-Century Vision*,   returns again and again
to details of Gustave Doré's   illustrations for "The Rime
of the Ancient Mariner," a poem   one is now tempted to read
as an environmental fable:

                               The arrogant mariner
who slays the albatross   is morally rudderless, off course,
his heart "dry as dust."   Only when he overcomes his revulsion
at the "thousand thousand   slimy things" around him, and sees
the beauty of the strange ocean beasts,   is he released
from his "death-in-life" and saved.   Now he roams the earth, haranguing
heedless revelers, forcing them to hear   that they must learn to love
"all creatures great and small."

                              Coleridge, anticipating Arnold,
was appalled   at the encroaching specter of modernity:
"the crash of onset; fear and rage....   Carnage and groans...the owlet
Atheism, sailing on obscene wings   across the noon."
He wished he could repel the impious invaders: "Render them
back upon the insulted ocean."   Like Arnold, he retreated
from the coming "evil days"   to his "own lowly cottage,"
his wife and child and "green and silent dell."

Despite Haeckel's
resolute atheism,   Coleridge might have discovered in him
a kindred spirit. Each in his own way   found "God in nature,"
and both might also have enjoyed   a seaside stroll with Shin
Kubota, featured   in the cover story of a recent
New York Times magazine,   who keeps in petri dishes
in "a small refrigerator"   "the world's only captive
population of immortal jellyfish."
He works alone
in Shinahama ("white beach"),   "a town full of timeless
natural wonders that are   failing the test of time."
Coastal erosion is rapidly   washing the beaches away;
now the white sand   is shipped in from Australia, and "a sublime
arched sandstone formation   that looks like a doughnut dunked halfway
into a glass of milk" is kept from collapse   by a scaffold and
"a harness of mortar and grout."
Kubota showed a reporter
how he induces a mature   jellyfish to "age in reverse."
Using two "fine metal picks,"   he repeatedly perforates
its delicate bell ("the size of a trimmed   pinkie fingernail"),
stabbing fifty times, until the creature   is "a depleted
gelatinous mass"   that looks "like an amoeba." It "folds
in on itself,   assuming the jellyfish equivalent
of the fetal position."
It is motionless, but the cells
are busy becoming younger,   presexual, all potential,
once again not yet   committed to particular roles.
They rest, regress, retool, and soon   they're ready to start again.
"By the end of the week,   stolons had begun to shoot
out of the meatball."   Kubota believes that once we grasp
how this "reversible   metamorphosis" works, "we will
become immortal ourselves."

But he warns, "Before we achieve
immortality, we must evolve first.   The heart is not good.
Human beings must learn to love nature.   Today the countryside
is obsolete.... We are in the garbage.   If this continues,
nature will die."   He uses karaoke to spread his message
in dozens of catchy songs,   such as "Die-Hard *Medusa*,"
"Life Forever," and "Living Planet—   Connections Between Forest,
Sea and Rural Area."

Haeckel was a showman, too.
He debated his opponents   in enormous lecture halls
packed with audiences eager   for an intellectual brawl.
He might have been taken aback   at Kubota's "superhero
alter ego, Mr. Immortal   Jellyfish Man," who appears
in "a red rubber hat   designed to resemble a *medusa*,
with dangling rubber tentacles,"   but he would have approved
of bringing science to the public.

And as a fellow-
medusologist, passionate   about the sea and some
of its least-   respected inhabitants, Haeckel surely
would have agreed with Kubota   that we need to focus on
what we have in common   with *medusae*. "The mystery
of life is not concealed   in the higher animals.
It is concealed in the root.   And at the root of the Tree
of Life is the jellyfish."

Haeckel believed that humans advance
as, one by one, "mysteries" are   demystified by science.
In his "extraordinary   *succès de scandale*," *Die Welträthsel*
(*The World Puzzles* or   *The Riddle of the Universe*), he argues
that there are no "transcendental problems."   Even ethics,
"the natural commandments   of sympathy and altruism"
are based "in the sexual love   and parental care upon which
the preservation of the species rests."

For all the scorn
he heaped on the "poetic conceit"   of the immortal soul,
Haeckel was not immune   to the "necessity of emotion...
the hope of seeing once more   the dear and loved ones whom death
has torn from us."   Lonely and embittered at sixty-four,
he was restored to life   by a new great love, and his suggestion
that this was a case of metempsychosis   may not have been
entirely in jest.

Frida von Uslar-Gleichen was born
the year Anna died,   and seemed to be "a reincarnation
of his first wife."   She wrote to him after reading his work, and soon
they were corresponding constantly   (over nine hundred pages
of their letters have been published   as *The Unsolved Riddle
of the Universe*), but "tied up in   a fraying Victorian
mentality," they spent only twenty-six   scattered, treasured,
secret days together.

He could not leave his "poor unhappy
second wife—a born Vestal virgin,"   but Frida "brought him back
into the living presence of Anna."   He sent her keepsakes
he had saved for thirty-four years: Anna's handkerchiefs, her handbag,
her jewelry (including   a four-piece engagement set, with blue pearls
and tiny iridescent shells),   an ivory box that held
a threadpaper in the shape   of a *medusa*, and a blank book
embossed in silver with the word *Poesie*.

She was his ideal,
"a symbol of his science and his art."   He wanted to end
Art Forms in Nature with her image,   "the apotheosis
of evolutionary thought":   a naked nymph, classically posed,
a jungle Snow White, lovely   but oddly small and featureless
compared to the vivid primate entourage   that encircles her:
seven anthropoid apes, perched in the trees   over her head, hanging
from the branches, and sprawled at her feet.

Frida disliked the picture.
"Beloved, couldn't you   present the female figure
on the last plate (plate 100!!) of your work   *without* apes?"
His publisher also protested, afraid   of a scandal.
Haeckel withdrew the plate;   he usually took Frida's advice,
saying she was his *Egeria*—   the water nymph, counselor,
and consort who taught   Emperor Pompilius Numa of Rome
justice and wisdom.
                    She said he was her Odysseus—
her sea-wanderer. If so,   he replied, she was Circe,
but unlike Homer's hero,   he had no desire to resist
his enchantress's charms.   Their epistolary effusions
are sometimes reminiscent of H.D.'s   *Notes on Thought and Vision*,
written after Bryher rescued her   from "the wreckage"
of her marriage,   and took her to the Scilly Islands "to be
healed by the wild sea."
                    In what Gelpi calls a "somewhat inchoate
mixture of seemingly   rational discriminations
and mythic invocations,"   she describes those "epiphanal"
moments when all "the polarities   seemed to fall away."
"The minds of two lovers merge, interact   in sympathy of thought.
The brain, inflamed   and excited by this interchange
of ideas, takes on its character   of overmind, becomes...
a jelly-fish, placed over and about the brain.
                    The love-region...
its energy not dissipated in   physical relation...
becomes this womb-brain or love-brain...   a jelly-fish *in* the body....
The love-mind and the over-mind   are two lenses. When these lenses
are properly adjusted, focused,   they bring the world of vision
into consciousness.   The two work separately, perceive separately,
yet make one picture."   Tragically, for Haeckel, this ecstatic
love-doubled vision did not last long.

His second "soul-bride"
also died young.   Frida's heart weakened; she was in terrible pain.
She begged him to send her more and more   morphine, which she finally
used for "self-deliverance."   Less austerely materialist
than Haeckel, she might have liked   H.D.'s mystical description
of the natural cycle, and of death as release: "This thistle—
life, love, martyrdom . . .   must lead in the logical course of events
to death, paradise, peace.

That world of death—that is death to the stings
of life, which is the highest life,   may be symbolised
by the serpent. . . . In my personal   language or vision, I call
this serpent a jelly-fish."   Jellyfish, serpent, cosmos,
Plato's revolving spherical   *ur*-universe, eternal
return, the self-devouring worm   Ouroboros—the terms
change but the concept persists: a constant, all-encompassing,
creative, destructive flux.

One might even reconcile this view
with Haeckel's notion of *Substance*:   the diverse phenomena
we label *space* and *time*, *matter* and *mind*,   are all aspects
of "the only   possible *perpetuum mobile*":
the "infinite and   eternal 'machine of the universe'"—
one oceanic flow.   "Substance is everywhere and always
uninterrupted   movement and transformation. Nowhere is there
perfect repose and rigidity."

Frida's body
lives on in whatever organisms   absorbed it; her spirit
lives on in her letters, and her name   lives on in yet another
medusa: *Rhopilema frida*,   which Haeckel discovered
in the Malaccan Strait.   Constant Roux translated his engravings
into glass—a chandelier   with scores of shimmering mouth-arms
and tentacles, that greets   visitors to the Museum
of Oceanography in Monaco.

Since Haeckel's time, tidelines
have crept higher as ocean levels rise.   This Halloween
much of New York was a ghost town,   blacked out by a hurricane.
The stars reflected in the flooded streets   were the only lights.
Fractured cranes dangled over construction sites.   Lewis's turbines,
his "uncompromising" Vortex, "proud   of its polished sides,"
which "insists on water-tight   compartments," might or might not
have survived.

In 1919, the year Haeckel died, H.D.,
in her offshore retreat,   reflected gloomily on human
mental habits: "All of our minds   are like dull little houses
built more or less alike,   a dull little city with rows
of little detached villas.   Each comfortable little home
shelters a comfortable little soul   and a wall at the back
shuts out completely   any communication
with the world beyond."

Why live like the nautilus, hunched
in a "sunless crypt"? Why not drift,   shell-less, skinless, "only a shade
more substantial than the water,"   wherever the ever-
wandering, ever-returning   ocean carries you?
Haeckel eagerly imagined the day   when we would be released
from the prison of received religion   into "the limitless
beauty that flows in inexhaustible streams   from the womb of our
Mother Nature."

As the twentieth century progressed,
he predicted, Goethe's noble   "philosophy of unity"
would prevail   over the "mystic and anthropistic
dogmas" of the past.   Obviously, this optimistic forecast
was not realized.   As Siebers observes, "In modern as well
as primitive societies,   the obstinate sacred
is not easily expelled,   and quickly climbs back over the walls
of our social and theoretical fortresses."

Today
the war rages on,   with battles in arenas high and low,
and Haeckel might be tickled   to learn that concerned citizens
of a new cyber realm he had never imagined   still view him
as a threat: the personification   of modern godlessness
and moral decay.   Groups such as answersingenesis.org
denounce Haeckel's "defraud of evidence."   "Did you know
that Haeckel frauded the pictures?"

They see his insistence
on the manifest fact   that, early in their embryonic
development, all species   look almost exactly alike
as a blasphemous attempt to erase   the divinely ordained
distinction between humans and the lesser beasts.   "Worse yet,
abortionists have long used   Haeckel's embryonic falsehood
to assuage the guilt of women,   telling them they're only
removing a fish."

Creation Ministries International
has posted many articles   like "Ernst Haeckel: Evangelist
for Evolution and Apostle   of Deceit," arguing that,
in addition to supplying an excuse   "for the slaughter
of millions of pre-natal children…   Haeckel provided
the malign influence   and pernicious inspiration that were
the indirect cause of two world wars   and the atrocities
of the Holocaust."

His academic attackers are just
as fanatical.   Gasman has devoted much of his career
to asserting that Haeckel was practically   single-handedly
responsible for the Decline of the West.   "Haeckel embraced death
and the meaninglessness   of human existence." Gasman's list
of Haeckel's evil progeny   includes (inter alia)
fascism, Marxism,   expressionism, euthanasia,
Dada, eugenics, and the Fauves.

According to Gasman,
Haeckel's work was the basis   for the elitist theories
of Le Bon, who claimed that crowds   "biogenetically revert
to 'primitive' forms   of behavior and expression,"
and of Gumplowicz, author of *Der Rassenkampf*,   who denied
autonomous thought: "It is not   man himself who thinks
but his social community;   the source of his thoughts
is the social medium in which he lives."

                                   But surely this is
in large part true,   and one need not be a fascist to worry
about the power of *idées reçues*,   which do not always
serve progress or the general good.   Lewis, too, had a horror
of crowds: "In ponderous masses, they prowl,   with excited hearts.
Are the Crowds then female?"   The throngs that converged in
    London and "roared
approval of the declaration   of war in 1914
were a jellyfish, in my judgment."

                                   Lewis probably meant
a siphonophore: "a cluster   of jellyfish" that "grow
together so intimately   that the nutritive juices
actually do stream into all of them   through a common axis."
(The deadly Portuguese   man o' war is the most famous species.)
Bölsche compares this "many-   animalled animal"
to "a bouquet, a colony,   a social community
or whatever you will. . . .

                                   They present themselves to the seaman
in the tropical ocean . . .   their large floats the size of a child's head
lying on the mirror of the water   like chased silver,
glinting violet and purple   from the blue of the sky
and crowned with a crest of brilliant carmine."   Each constituent
of these "polymorphic persons"   is an organ of the great
"medusa-state,"   illustrating what Haeckel called the "splendid
law of division

of labor," "the indispensable
foundation on which the existence   and effectiveness
of the whole group rests."   Even in Eden, "Adam delved and Eve span,"
and when hominids divided up the chores,   life improved.
"Each man" (as Plato put it)   should pursue "a craft for which
he was naturally fitted."   The wise should rule; the brave should
    wage war;
the dexterous should produce clothing and tools;   and the useless
poets, who "opine contraries at the same time,"

should be banished.
Similarly, in the sea,   ancient independent hydroids
evolved into "citizens"   of a siphonophore republic:
one eats, one reproduces, one inflates the sail,   and one kills
prey and enemies.   The "chief polyp," "like a central soup kitchen,"
impartially dispenses   "a Spartan broth" of nutrients,
and the community prospers.   But is each of these specialized
"persons" a person, or part of a person?

The field was split.
Attempting, as usual,   to reconcile opposing views,
Haeckel sought a middle ground   between the "poly-person"
and the "poly-organ" positions.   His Medusome theory
outlines the organic   differentiation process
by which colonial entities   come to be both unified
and divided, with each   "person" reliving in miniature
the history of the species.

He performed experiments
on siphonophore larvae   (anticipating current research
on totipotent cells),   showing that changes in the environment
affect development,   and that early embryos, cut apart,
can regenerate.   Like Plato's smooth, round, newborn universe,
"sufficient unto itself,"   containing both "Sameness
and Difference," the first   new siphonophore cell holds the germs
of all its potential later forms.

Furthermore, siphonophores
have "a double soul: the *personal soul* of the numerous
individualities which compose them,   and the common
harmoniously acting psyche   of the entire colony."
Haeckel even argued that "every cell...   is to some extent
an independent being,"   with a "cell-soul" of its own.
Some humans balk here,   correctly suspecting an analogy
with themselves.

Since Haeckel's day, we have more or less accepted
that the anthill is a "superorganism,"   that the beehive
buzzes with communal purpose,   and that our own bodies
consist almost wholly   of innumerable tiny creatures,
living their own invisible lives.   Still, humans value
autonomy and are usually   made uneasy by
beings that "challenge us to think about   what we mean when we call
something an individual."

Dunn notes that "an Amoeba,
which is a solitary cell,   would have much the same
problem contemplating   the individuality
of a human," but that's no great consolation.   We don't want
to think of ourselves as just the sum   of our organs, much less
of the millions of tiny wills   in our microbiomes.
Nor do we want to be   a cog in some vast, collective
cognitive machine.

Lewis's "Crowd-Master," a writer,
ventures experimentally   into the thronging street. "He sank
like a diver.... Soon he had become   an entranced medium,"
and with *"authentic shock,"* he finds   he has "penetrated its mind—
the cerebration of this jellyfish!   Hence the sting!
It seemed to be that he   was a *married* man." Revolted,
he withdraws from the "human lake"   that induced *"that married
    feeling"*
into a bar and orders "a bitter beer."

                              If immersion
in the moist over-intimacy   of the mass mind sickens
Lewis's masterman,   how would a lesser specimen react
to having his thoughts hijacked   by an extraterrestrial hive-brain?
In Sturgeon's *To Marry Medusa*   (a.k.a. *The Cosmic Rape*),
Gurlick, "a scrubby, greasy,   rotten-toothed near-illiterate,"
scrounges a "sodden and slippery"   half-eaten hamburger
from a garbage can,

                         and ingests the encysted alien spore
of "the Medusa, the galactic man o' war,   the super-
consciousness of the illimitable beast."   It has conquered
"two galaxies and part of a third,"   but has "never encountered
intelligence, except   as a phenomenon of the group."
Why can't it connect,   through Gurlick, directly with every human?
It concludes that *Homo sapiens*'   brain must have fragmented
defensively, "like the chipmunk's tail,

                                        the sea cucumber's
ejectible intestines."   Gurlick serves as a clumsy verbal
intermediary, asking everyone,   "How could we get
all put together again?"   Soon the Medusa has learned enough
to build an enhanced encephalogram,   joining all human minds,
but its conquest will not be complete   until it consummates
"its marriage to humanity";   Gurlick's "altered seed"
must penetrate a "welcoming ovum."

                              And so it comes to pass.
His favorite fantasy   is realized; the "decent, pleated, skirted"
repressed spinster Dimity   ("No cesspool for her") is transformed;
she reclaims her original name: Salomé, which "reflected
all the luminance of wickedness and sin."   Gurlick watches her
"swimming now naked in the sun   sure and fearless, shameless."
When she wades towards him, saying, "Hello, Handsome,"   it's
   finally time
for his "special chore."

"Never before and never again
would marriage occur with such explosion... the Medusa of space
shot down its contacting thread, an unerring harpoon carrying
a line to itself, and all of its Self following in the line,
ready to reach and fill humanity, making of it
a pseudopod, the newest member of its sprawling corpus."
But the noble force of individuality defeats
communal compliance.

When the Medusa invades our species,
free will "flooded it, filled it to its furthermost crannies, drenched
its most remote cells with the Self of humankind. Die? Never that.
The Medusa was alive as never before... its slaves were free
but its motivations unified." A new sort of being
is born: "star-man, the immeasurable, the limitless,
the growing, maker of music beyond music, poetry
beyond words...."

In an instant, the galactic superconsciousness
is democratized, and Salomé, unlike her biblical
namesake, does not demand the hero's head. "Ideal antagonists,
ideal weapons in the conflict between Medusa and mankind,"
she and Gurlick go forth, conversing wordlessly, "in a sort
of semaphore of the emotions," into a new Eden.
"Medusa had won the battles; mankind had won the war,"
and Gurlick had made it possible.

The "sentient immensity
acknowledged to him its debt... his desires would be fulfilled."
He was just "a minor atom in a simple molecule
of a primitive cell," but he remained "a free agent,"
and "you do not reward a catalyst by changing it."
Gurlick's essence is suffering, greed, and rage, so Paradise,
in order not to "emasculate him," still holds one small
patch of urban squalor for him to hate.

Maybe writers
of science fiction,   like scientists, are less distressed
than humanists at the prospect   of collective cognition.
For Barthes, the barbed tentacle   linking the individual
to the masses is toxic.   He compares the paralyzing
effects of *Doxa*, public opinion,   to those of both the real
and the mythical Medusa: "castration...   I am in a stunned
state, dazed, cut off from the popularity of language."

Once,
he was pressured into swimming   in "a cold sea, infested"
with *medusae*.   "I was one of a group, which justifies
any cowardice."   He emerged "covered with stings and blisters,"
and swabbed himself with potassium chloride.   After exposure
to the noxious "products   of mass culture," the intellectual,
"constantly listening to what   I am excluded from," requires
a comparable "detergent discourse."

Medusa "is *evident*,"
but not directly seen,   "a gelatinous mass which sticks
onto the retina," obscuring vision.   Why, then, are we
drawn to her irresistibly?   Barthes, "a man of paradox,
like any writer," reminds us   that she is "a caricature";
Athena has curdled her loveliness. Thus,   "in the *Doxa*'s
discourse there are former beauties sleeping,   the memory
of a once sumptuous and fresh wisdom."

Indeed, Athena,
the armor-plated virgin, whom Murnaghan   calls "the entirely
reassuring and unseductive...   female upholder
of male-dominated social structures,"   is Medusa's
virtuous twin.   Bearing a shield that portrays the severed head
of the gorgon, she fights in support   of "the imposition
of order on natural forces,"   especially the ocean,
"whose unruliness Poseidon leaves unchecked."

                                         Moreover, her birth
fully clad from the head of Zeus   (who had swallowed her mother)
recalls the emergence of Pegasus,   sired by Poseidon,
from the Medusa's severed neck.   Athena, tamer of horses,
helped Bellerophon bridle,   mount, and ride the immortal
white-winged stallion that eventually   evolved into a symbol
of deathless verse and the power   of the imagination to soar,
transporting the earthbound bard.
                              Social order or chaos? Blind
acceptance of received ideas   or the terrifying truth?
Is Medusa the scapegoat that must be slain   for the good of the group,
or hoi polloi itself,   the many headed, hissing mob?
In Cellini's great statue,   Perseus stands proudly astride
the dead gorgon, brandishing   her head, his potent trophy.
"The hero's tangled locks,"   Siebers notices, "mimic the coils
of the serpents that entwine the victim's head."
                                  The two profiles
"fuse into one." For Siebers,   the gorgon is the unfortunate
human tendency to "divide   their group and the sacred in two...
representing identities   as differences.... The seemingly
antithetical figures   of Medusa and Athena
are only two different expressions   made by the same face.
Once we detach our view   from the mythological perspective
of the community
                     the difference between the divinity
and the monster vanishes."   Siebers's gorgon is like Barthes's
Medusa of public opinion   (and the antithesis
of H.D.'s revelatory jellyfish lens):   an "evil eye"
which saps our power,   distorts our perceptions, and leaves us confused
and woozy, a bit   like the way we feel after a stint
in the hermeneutic   hall of mirrors: that infinite
regression of reflections of....

Oh please—no more *mises en abyme*!
No more aporias!   You're sick of specularity, the gaze,
paradox, mediation,   "phallogocentric sublation,"
and all the other magic formulas   that turn living myths
into didactic statues   with hectoring wall texts urging you
to scourge yourself for a host of unconscious   atavistic sins:
"an ancient tale of wrong,   Like a tale of little meaning
tho' the words are strong."

Eliot was right that "The sea
is all about us," but it doesn't have to be   all about *us*.
"The sea was not a mask. No more   was" that jellyfish
that collided limply with your naked thigh   a metaphor.
Leave it in the water, alive.   "You put it on a piece
of blotting paper and it dries up   into the spectral
outline of a shadow, a tiny   fat-spot, summary
of its whole existence."

So shut that book! "Always afternoon"
won't last forever.   Pack a cooler full of lotos,
come out of your ivory cell,   take off your shoes, and stroll
along the strand, feeling the spent surf   fizzle around your toes.
Then set up a beach umbrella and doze   in "dreamful ease...
with half-dropt eyelid still,"   beside "this distant northern sea,"
letting "the grating roar   of the pebbles which the waves draw back"
draw you back to an ancient shore.

You are Perseus, triumphant.
Your bronze torso gleams.   The dreadful head is safely packed away
in the Hesperides' sack.   You have turned your enemy
into a weapon.   Now you can rescue Andromeda, your bride,
from the rock where she lies shackled,   yet another sacrifice
to insatiable Poseidon....   The monster is dead, but the story
isn't over; it seems   you have been both executioner
and midwife. Something in there

is moving—a muzzle, a hoof,
a foreleg, a haunch—a white horse   (enormous, impossible!
and what are those feathers unfolding from the shoulders?)   is thrusting
up out of the neck stump.   Pegasus rears and whinnies, pulls free
of the gorgon corpse,   and soars away, shaking thick, wine-dark drops
of Medusa blood from his snowy   Apollonian wings.
They fall into Okeanus,   "whence is sprung the seed
of all the immortals,"

and the cycle starts again. Perhaps,
as Lewis somewhat puzzlingly asserts,   "the *artist*
is older than the fish,"   and constantly takes on new forms
to adapt to new conditions.   Or maybe art itself came first.
Protean, parthenogenetic,   the *ur*-myth buds, propagates
and evolves in "the reservoir of the soul."   The would-be
gorgon slayer watches helplessly,   hovering between sea
and sky, as Hesiod says, "like a thought in the mind,"

"The mind,
that ocean, where each kind   Does straight its own resemblance find."
Marvell's garden, too, has its submarine   double: H.D.'s
"sea-garden," which, in Haeckel's words, "exceeds   by far the fabled
gardens of the Hesperides....   The blue deep is overheaped
with blossoms, bloom atop bloom, and each   a living creature....
Glittering metallic fish flash by,   like the hummingbirds that feed
at the throats of tropical plants."

Haeckel didn't believe
in the Hesperides. But even as he   argued that the richness
of the real world surpasses   our most fervid fantasies,
he relied on myth.   The "Daughters of the Night" dwell at the rim
of the ocean-girdled earth,   guarding the "Tree of Life," whose golden
"apples of joy and discord" were stolen   by Strife, to cause the Fall
of Troy and the trials of Odysseus,   and by Herakles
to attain immortality.

Now that would be a worthy quest!
No mortal has ever returned   from the land where the "Sunset
Goddesses" tend their fruit,   and only Proteus knows the route.
You could wrestle him for the secret,   build a mighty boat
"that the water would never go through,"   lash yourself to the mast
and set off westward, singing,   "I am the captain of my soul . . .
and a right good captain, too."   Maybe you could make Poseidon
turn the tide around, just for you.

                                            No, you are not King Canute,
nor were meant to be, and the sirens   have retired. So get down
from your flimsy throne,   strip off your grandfather's clumsy
armor, and swim   until you're far over your head in the *hungry*,
dark-heaving sea, "an imaginary   garden with real"
jellyfish. They wash past you,   "scarcely a particle
of solidity in them,   defying the water world
which can snap your huge steamer like a reed."

                                            Scylla, Charybdis,
fog, iceberg, reef,   a misread chart, a dozing helmsman, a U-boat,
one good blow   from an annoyed Aeolus, one seismic rumble
that slowly but surely swells   into an enormous, hubris-
smashing tsunami,   and down goes the *Lusitania*,
the *Deutschland*, nuns and all,   the frigate *Medusa*. You're left
clutching a rickety raft,   nervously sizing up your fellow
lucky survivors.

                        You're on your own. Neither Athena
nor any kindly fisherman   will scoop you back to safety.
In the *Times*, a geneticist   optimistically proposes,
"Immortality may be   much more common than we thought,"
and Kubota believes "it will be easy   to solve the mystery
of immortality and apply   ultimate life
to human beings." But if   this ever actually happens,
it will be after your time.

Haeckel asserts that "humanity
is but a transitory phase   of the evolution of an
eternal substance," a statement in which   one catches a whiff
of the very teleology   he so often dismissed.
He could never completely abandon   the idea of progress.
Replacing "the adoration   of old clothes and wax dolls"
with monism would be a step   forward in "the historical
development of the soul of man."
                              "In the 'new faith,' poetry
and the cultivation of the beautiful   will be called upon
to play a greater role than ever."   In fact, at times the language
of the most hard-nosed materialists   slips oddly into
a vertiginous metaphysical   diction akin to
the mystics'.   Bölsche says, "We are momentary waves
on the infinite ocean of life";   John of Damascus
says, "God is a sea of infinite substance";

                              and in *Monism
as Connecting Religion and Science*,   Haeckel, the heretic,
says, "God is everywhere...the sum   of all atomic forces
and all ether vibrations."   He exhorts his readers to "advance
towards the solution   of the fundamental riddle
of the universe"   through "the reconciliation of
apparent antitheses":   body and soul, multiplicity
and unity, death and life.
                              It's worth a try. You've always known
that "your goal was a shoal,"   that one day "your bower of bone"
would crumble, so get ready for what comes next.   Practice your role
as "an insignificant part   in an all-embracing world-soul."
Relax into the ineluctable   flux, in a willing
suspension of belief.   You didn't come into this world
from another, "trailing   clouds of glory," but from this one, imbued
with an enduring elemental force,

which will have to do.
This impersonal immortality   has its own appeal.
Think yourself back and forth   from the *wrinkled, briny, perfumed*
womb of your "great sweet mother,   Mother and lover of men, the sea,"
into "a distant future   in which most other species of life
are extinct, but the ocean will consist   overwhelmingly
of immortal jellyfish,   a great gelatin consciousness
everlasting."

                    Or transitory. If we're really heading back
to "a system reminiscent   of the Cambrian era,"
maybe it's a way of making a fresh start.   The algae blooms
that have smothered other life-forms   are ambrosia for jellyfish.
They feed and spawn, even unto   the millionth generation,
when some random   misfolded protein may result in a new
knot in a nerve net, which then   may be favored by a change
in the atmosphere, so the knot remains,

                                        repeats; more knots
accumulate in a sort   of living *quipu*, a record
of the species' eons-long,   perilous, wave-tossed journey
from reflex to thought.   One day, *medusa* bards may sing
of the sweet salt billows of heaven   and the parched tortures of hell,
and praise the supreme power that clearly   loves jellyfish best,
and has therefore provided   the perfect environment
for their triumphal ascent.
                        Where are you in this scenario?
Maybe humans   have ascended, too. Maybe you're a long-haul
astronaut, navigating   intergalactic abysses
in a little capsule.   Your *Michelin Guide to the Milky Way*
beeps three times: Point of Interest coming up starboard, quadrant A.
Ah yes, "the Blue Planet."   You remember that from history class.
Mich reads you a line   from a protoextraorbital
writer, Arthur C. Clarke:

            "How inappropriate to call
this planet Earth when it   is clearly ocean." That's true—
look at it glistening!   The globe-enfolding *medusa* membrane
creates a pearly sheen   on the face of the waters.
MichPix shows you close-ups: the major archipelagos: Alps,
Andes, Himalayas, and,   at maximum magnification,
you think you can even see hints   of some of the monuments
pictured in Archive:
                Machu Picchu, Burj Khalifa, the Great Wall,
the Pyramids, Googopolis, Fresh Kills . . .   dark flecks, like old splinters
under the gently   undulating jelly-skin. They're still
prime real estate—an excellent substrate   for polyp colonies.
Many travelers have found images   to capture this view:
"a robin's egg," "an azulisphere,"   "a Cyclopean eye,
all blue iris, glossed with cataract,   staring dimly back at me
as I fly by."
       Those who know the history of Terra
naturally picture "a luminous   blue *medusa*, afloat in
a midnight ocean." A poet offers a haiku: "The party
goes on. / No one even notices   / the escaped balloon."
A biologist sees "an isolated cell   suspended
in a dark medium,   waiting for someone to tease out a phrase
of its encrypted narrative,   or, far more likely, to fail,
wash it off the slide, and start again."
                      It's gone. Or rather
you're gone. You've passed it, and a sudden   rough "caress of wave"
jolts you awake.   You've splashed back down into the present; the sun
is lower now. "The long day wanes . . . the deep   Moans round with
    many voices,"
so join the chorus.   Even the dyspeptic Lewis says, "Bless
all seafarers. They exchange not one   land for another, but one
element for another, the more   against the less abstract.
Bless the vast planetary abstraction of the OCEAN."

Yes.
It's pleasant not   always to be solid, pleasant to be a dot
riding the wavery line between two blues,   feeling it now and then
nearly disappear   over and under you as you cruise,
fugitive, native, embraced, exposed   in "the strangeness of the sea."
It's pleasant to be a floating oxymoron,   or less—a word,
"more verb than noun," or just a syllable   of a language whose
syntax is too complex for you to grasp.

Parse one segment
and the parts have already   realigned into a new
transient sentence.   The most you can hope for is that two
agreeable syllables, bobbing on   the "staunching, quenching
ocean of a motionable mind,"   will, from time to time,
happen to lap   up against each other, adding a rhyme,
to the "milky, star-infused   Poem / of the sea . . . stronger
than alcohol, vaster than our lyres."

And the sea, in its turn,
eternally rhymes with the sky.   The "gaseous vertebrate"
and the rest of the capricious specters   may have been almost
exorcised from "this celestial seascape,"   but as you ride the tide,
letting your thoughts mimic "its mimic motion,"   the "sovereign
    clouds,"
like ghosts of ghosts,   persistently seduce you into seeing
possible pictures: "iconopoesis . . . mimesis
of an invisible original."

Like poor Gurlick
with the Medusa's "wrinkled milt . . . lying like a metrical
lesion on the inner surface   of his mind," you're just a "host-
integer" for the sleeping spore   of a "gigantic cognizance,"
and your best ideas just the "tropistic   flailings of something
amputated." What can you do?   Join the lotos-eaters? "Muse
and brood" in a placid limbo of denial?   "Let what is broken
so remain. The Gods are hard to reconcile."

But "meditation
and water," says Melville, "are wedded   forever." For a while,
you can float on "a slumberous sheet   of foam," your extended
    feelers
oscillating, making occasional   lazy water angels
on "the concave firmament."   You can imagine what it's like
to be yourself: "a little wash'd-up drift,"   a speck
of protoplasm on "the glorious mirror,"   a fleeting speech
bubble on the *unexhaustible   much-echoing ocean.*

BIBLIOGRAPHY

Albrecht, Thomas. *The Medusa Effect*. Albany: SUNY Press, 2009.

Barthes, Roland. "The Jellyfish 'Medusa' and the Power to Stun." In *The Medusa Reader*, edited by Marjorie Garber and Nancy J. Vickers, 131–32. New York: Routledge, 2003.

Benjamin, Walter. "Medusa and Modernity." In *The Medusa Reader*, edited by Marjorie Garber and Nancy J. Vickers, 89. New York: Routledge, 2003.

Bölsche, Wilhelm. *Haeckel, His Life and Work*. Translated by Joseph Mc-Cabe. Philadelphia, PA: George W. Jacobs & Co., 1906.

_____. *Love-Life in Nature*. 2 vols. Translated by Cyril Brown. New York: Albert & Charles Boni, 1926.

Breidbach, Olaf. *Visions of Nature: The Art and Science of Ernst Haeckel*. Munich: Prestel, 2006.

Conan Doyle, Arthur, Sir. *The Case-Book of Sherlock Holmes*. New York: Oxford University Press, 1999.

Connor, Judith L., and Nora L. Deans. *Jellies: Living Art*. Monterey, CA: Monterey Bay Aquarium Foundation, 2002.

De Casseres, Benjamin. "Jules de Gaultier: Super-Nietzschean." *The Forum* 49 (January 1913): 86–90. Quoted in Per Petersen, "Jack London's Medusa of Truth." *Philosophy and Literature* 26, no. 1 (2002). Proquest, accessed November 8, 2011.

Di Gregorio, Mario A. *From Here to Eternity: Ernst Haeckel and Scientific*

Faith. Vol. 3 of *Religion, Theology and Natural Science*. Göttingen: Vandenhoek and Ruprecht, 2005.

H.D. [Hilda Doolittle]. *Collected Poems, 1912–1944*. New York: New Directions, 1986.

_____. *Notes on Thought and Vision*. San Francisco: City Lights Books, 1982.

Dumoulié, Camille. "Medusa in Myth and Literary History." In *Companion to Literary Myths, Heroes and Archetypes*, edited by Pierre Brunel. New York: Routledge, 1966. www.english.illinois.edu/maps/poets/a_f/bogan/medusamyth.htm, accessed June 24, 2012.

Dunn, Casey. "Siphonophores." n.d. www.siphonophores.org/SiphOrganization.php, accessed July 10, 2013.

Eliot, T. S. "Tar." *The Egoist* 5/6 (June–July 1918): 84. Quoted in Scott W. Klein, introduction to *Tarr*, by Wyndham Lewis. Oxford: Oxford World Classics, 2010

Ernst-Haeckel-Haus der Universität Jena. Museum guide from *"museum"* series. Braunschweig: Westermann, n.d.

Euripides. "The Power of Gorgon's Blood." In *The Medusa Reader*, edited by Marjorie Garber and Nancy J. Vickers, 16–19. New York: Routledge, 2003.

Fischer, Martin, Gunnar Brehm, and Uwe Hoßfeld. *Das Phyletische Museum in Jena*. Jena: Institut für Spezielle Zoologie und Evolutionsbiologie mit Phyletischem Museum, 2008.

Foshay, Toby. *Wyndham Lewis and the Avant-Garde: The Politics of the Intellect*. Montreal: McGill-Queens University Press, 1992.

Freud, Sigmund. "Medusa's Head." In *The Medusa Reader*, edited by Marjorie Garber and Nancy J. Vickers, 84–85. New York: Routledge, 2003.

Garber, Marjorie, and Nancy J. Vickers, eds. *The Medusa Reader*. New York: Routledge, 1903.

Gąsiorek, Andrzej. *Wyndham Lewis and Modernism*. Horndon, Devon: Northcote House, 2004.

Gasman, Daniel. *Haeckel's Monism and the Birth of Fascist Ideology*. New York: Peter Lang, 1998.

Gelpi, Albert. Introduction. In H.D. [Hilda Doolittle], *Notes on Thought and Vision*, 7–14. San Francisco: City Lights Books, 1982.

Grigg, Russell. "Ernst Haeckel: Evangelist for Evolution and Apostle of Deceit." *Creation Ministries International.* creation.com/ernst-haeckel-evangelist-for-evolution-and-apostle-of-deceit, accessed June 18, 2012.

Haeckel, Ernst. *Anthropogenie oder Entwicklungsgeschichte des Menschen.* Leipzig: Wilhelm Engelmann, 1903.

_____. *Arabische Korallen.* Berlin: Georg Reimer. Quoted in "Ernst-Haeckel-Haus der Universität Jena," *"museum"* (Braunschweig: Westermann, n.d.), 83–84.

_____. *Art Forms in Nature.* Translated by Michele Schons. Munich: Prestel, 2009.

_____. *Ewigkeit: Weltkriegsgedanken über Leben und Tod, Religion und Entwicklungslehre.* Berlin: Georg Reimer, 1915.

_____. *Himmelhoch Jauchzend: Erinnerungen und Briefe der Liebe.* Dresden: Carl Reissner, 1927.

_____. *The History of Creation.* Translated and revised by E. Ray Lankester. London: Kegan Paul, Trench Trübner & Co., 1899.

_____. *Italienfahrt: Briefe an die Braut, 1859/1860.* Leipzig: K. F. Koehler, 1921.

_____. *Monism as Connecting Religion and Science.* Translated by J. Gilchrist. London: Adam and Charles Black, 1895.

_____. *The Riddle of the Universe.* Translated by Joseph McCabe. New York: Harper & Brothers, 1900.

_____. *Das System der Medusen.* 2 vols. Jena: Gustav Fischer, 1879.

_____. "Ueber Arbeitstheilung in Natur- und Menschenleben." Lecture transcript. Berlin: C. G. Lüderit'sche Verlagsbuchhandlung, 1869.

Haeckel, Ernst, and Frida von Uslar-Gleichen. *Die ungelöste Welträtsel: Frida von Uslar-Gleichen und Ernst Haeckel, Briefe und Tagebücher 1898–1900.* Edited by Norbert Elsner. 3 vols. Göttingen: Wallstein, 2000.

"Haeckel Kills the Soul. From the London Telegraph." *The New York Times,* May 8, 1905, 8. Proquest Historical Newspapers (March 10, 1912).

Harper, Lila M. "'The Starfish that Burns': Gendering the Jellyfish." In *Forces of Nature: Natural(-ing) Gender and Gender(ing) Nature in the Discourses of Western Culture,* edited by Bernadette H. Hyner and Precious McKenzie Stearns, 21–50. Newcastle upon Tyne: Cambridge Scholars Publishing, 2009.

Hayward, Eva. "Sensational Jellyfish: Aquarium Affects and the Matter of Immersion." *differences: A Journal of Feminist Cultural Studies* 25, no. 3 (2012): 161–96.

Hesiod. "Medusa and Perseus." In *The Medusa Reader*, edited by Marjorie Garber and Nancy J. Vickers, 11–13. New York: Routledge, 2003.

Jones, William. *The Broad, Broad Ocean*. London: Frederick Warne and Co. 1871.

Krauße, Erika. *Ernst-Haeckel-Haus der Universität Jena*. Braunschweig: Westermann, 1990.

Lewis, Wyndham. *Blasting and Bombardiering*. Berkeley, CA: University of California Press, 1967.

_____. "Enemy of the Stars." *Blast* 1 (1914): 51–85.

_____. "Manifesto—I." *Blast* 1 (1914): 11–29.

_____. *Men Without Art*. New York: Russell & Russell, 1964.

_____. "Our Vortex." *Blast* 1 (1914): 147–49.

_____. *Tarr*. Oxford: Oxford World Classics, 2010.

_____. *Time and Western Man*. New York: Harcourt, Brace and Co., 1928.

_____. "Vortex. Pound." *Blast* 1 (1914): 153–54.

London, Jack. *The Mutiny of the Elsinore*. New York: Popular Library, 1960.

_____. *The Science Fiction Stories of Jack London*. Edited by James Bankes. New York: Carol Publishing Group, 1993.

Lovecraft, H. P. *Best Supernatural Stories*. Cleveland, OH: The World Publishing Company, 1945.

Marx, Karl. "The Medusa of Capital Production." In *The Medusa Reader*, edited by Marjorie Garber and Nancy J. Vickers, 77–78. New York: Routledge, 2003.

Mills, Claudia. "Jellyfish Blooms: Are Populations Increasing Globally in Response to Changing Ocean Conditions?" *Hydrobiologia* 451 (2001): 55–68.

Murnaghan, Sheila. "The Plan of Athena." In *The Distaff Side: Representing the Female in Homer's* Odyssey," edited by Beth Cohen, 61–80. New York: Oxford University Press, 1995.

Neumann, Erich. "A Jungian View of the Terrible Mother." In *The Medusa*

Reader, edited by Marjorie Garber and Nancy J. Vickers, 96–99. New York: Routledge, 2003.

Nietzsche, Friedrich. *Morgenröte*. Vol. 3 of *Kritische Studienausgabe*. Munich: Deutscher Taschenbuch Verlag, 1999.

_____. *Posthumous Fragments, Winter 1884–5*. Quoted in Camille Dumoulié, "Medusa in Myth and Literary History." In *Companion to Literary Myths, Heroes and Archetypes*, edited by Pierre Brunel. New York: Routledge, 1966. www.english.illinois.edu/maps/poets/a_f/bogan/medusamyth.htm, accessed June 24, 2012.

Parker, Valerie. "Enemies of the Absolute: Lewis, Art and Women." In *Wyndham Lewis: A Revaluation*, edited by Jeffrey Meyers, 211–25. London: Athlone Press, 1980.

Petersen, Per. "Jack London's Medusa of Truth." *Philosophy and Literature* 26, no. 1 (2002): 43–56. Proquest, accessed November 8, 2011.

Piraino, Stefano, Ferdinando Boero, Brigitte Aeschbach, and Volker Schmid. "Reversing the Life Cycle: Medusae Transforming into Polyps and Cell Transdifferentiation in *Turritopsis nutricula* (Cnidaria, Hyrozoa). *Biological Bulletin* 190 (June 1996): 302–12. JSTOR, accessed December 10, 2012.

Plato. *Plato's Timaeus*. Translated by Francis M. Cornfeld. New York: The Liberal Arts Press, 1959.

_____. *The Republic of Plato*. Translated by Allan Bloom. New York: Basic Books, 1968.

Proteus. Directed by David Lebrun. 60 min. Icarus Films, 2004.

Purcell, Jennifer, Shin-ichi Uye, and Wen-Tseng Lo. "Anthropogenic Causes of Jellyfish Blooms and Their Direct Consequences for Humans: A Review." *Marine Ecology Progress Series* 350 (2007): 1153–174.

Rich, Nathaniel. "Can a Jellyfish Unlock the Secret of Immortality?" *The New York Times Magazine*, November 28, 2012.

Richards, Robert. *The Tragic Sense of Life: Ernst Haeckel and the Struggle over Evolutionary Theory*. Chicago: University of Chicago Press, 2008.

Richardson, Anthony, Andrew Bakun, Graeme C. Hays, and Mark J. Gibbons. "The Jellyfish Joyride: Causes, Consequences and Management Responses to a More Gelatinous Future." *Trends in Ecology and Evolution* 24, no. 6 (2009): 312–22.

Rose, H. J. *A Handbook of Greek Mythology.* New York: Dutton, 1959.

Scott, Bonnie Kime. "Jellyfish and Treacle: Lewis, Joyce, Gender, and Modernism." In *Coping with Joyce,* edited by Morris Beja and Shari Benstock, 168–79. Columbus, OH: Ohio University Press, 1989.

Siebers, Tobin. *The Mirror of Medusa.* Berkele , CA: University of California Press, 1983.

Sturgeon, Theodore. *To Marry Medusa.* New York: Baen, 1987.

Than, Ker. "'Immortal' Jellyfish Swarm World's Oceans." *National Geographic News.* news.nationalgeographic.com/news/2009/01/090130-immortal-jellyfish-swarm.html, accessed January 29, 2009.

Whitaker, J. David, Rachel King, and David Knott. "Jellyfish." *Department of Natural Resources, South Carolina, Marine Resources Division,* 2010, www.dnr.sc.gov/marine/pub/seascience/jellyfi.html, accessed January 15, 2013.

Wylie, Philip. "Momism." In *The Medusa Reader,* edited by Marjorie Garber and Nancy J. Vickers, 90–91. New York: Routledge, 2003.

Earlier versions of some of the poems in this volume have appeared in the following publications:

The Antioch Review: "Twists"

The Baffler: "To Be Rid of a Rival"

Barrow Street: "Safety Measures"

Bomb: "To Cross Safely over Thin Ice"

Cimarron: "Night Patrol"

Columbia: "On the Graphic Representation of Time," "On the Metaphoric Impulse," "Pinocchio's Pleasures," "Pinocchio on Location"

Confrontation: "How to Locate"

Gargoyle: "Pinocchio on Wishes"

The Gettysburg Review: "The Touch," "Hole-Up"

Little Star: "Team"

Northwest Review: "For One Troubled by Internal Pain"

Parnassus: "Class Tip," "On the Accuracy of the Historical Record," "*Flashback:* Pinocchio Learns the Method," "Why Do Some Mediums Hide in Boxes?"

Pleiades: "Pipefest," "Ethics"

Ploughshares: "The Fix and the Fall"

A Public Space: "Contingent," "The Whiz Is Dying"

Raritan: "High Enlightenment," "On the Whiz," "The Frame," "Bundling—Its Origin, Progress, and Decline in America"

Smartish Pace: "Family Outfit," "Curdled Fix," "Knockabout"

DANTE ALIGHIERI The New Life
Translated by Dante Gabriel Rossetti; Preface by Michael Palmer

KINGSLEY AMIS Collected Poems: 1944–1979

GUILLAUME APOLLINAIRE Zone: Selected Poems
Translated by Ron Padgett

AUSTERITY MEASURES The New Greek Poetry
Edited by Karen Van Dyck

SZILÁRD BORBÉLY Berlin-Hamlet
Translated by Ottilie Mulzet

MARGARET CAVENDISH *Edited by Michael Robbins*

NAJWAN DARWISH Nothing More to Lose
Translated by Kareem James Abu-Zeid

BENJAMIN FONDANE Cinepoems and Others
Edited by Leonard Schwartz

W. S. GRAHAM *Selected by Michael Hofmann*

SAKUTARŌ HAGIWARA Cat Town
Translated by Hiroaki Sato

MICHAEL HELLER Telescope: Selected Poems

MIGUEL HERNÁNDEZ *Selected and translated by Don Share*

RYSZARD KRYNICKI Our Life Grows
Translated by Alissa Valles; Introduction by Adam Michnik

LOUISE LABÉ Love Sonnets and Elegies
Translated by Richard Sieburth

ALEXANDER VVEDENSKY An Invitation for Me to Think
Translated by Eugene Ostashevsky and Matvei Yankelevich

WALT WHITMAN Drum-Taps: The Complete 1865 Edition
Edited by Lawrence Kramer

ELIZABETH WILLIS Alive: New and Selected Poems